KALF The Korean Association for Local Finance  C&F System

Korean Local Finance

C&F Academic Series I

도서출판 윤성사 214

The Korean Association for Local Finance · C&F System
Korean Local Finance

제1판 제1쇄	2023년 12월 6일

지 은 이	B. Shine Cho, Hyungjo Hur, Jaewon Lee The Korean Association for Local Finance
기 획	The Korean Association for Local Finance·C&F System
펴 낸 이	정재훈
꾸 민 이	안미숙

펴 낸 곳	도서출판 윤성사
주 소	서울특별시 용산구 효창원로64길 10 백오빌딩 지하 1층
전 화	대표번호_02)313-3814 / 영업부_02)313-3813 / 팩스_02)313-3812
전자우편	yspublish@daum.net
등 록	2017. 1. 23

ISBN 979-11-93058-17-6 (93350)
값 15,000원

© The Korean Association for Local Finance, 2023

지은이와의 협의에 따라 인지를 생략합니다.

이 책의 전부 또는 일부 내용을 재사용하려면 반드시 사전에 저작권자와 도서출판 윤성사의 동의를 받아야 합니다.

잘못 만들어진 책은 구입하신 서점에서 교환 가능합니다.

C&F Academic Series I

Korean Local Finance

B. Shine Cho, Hyungjo Hur, Jaewon Lee
The Korean Association for Local Finance

Preface

Local Finance is the theory, system, and policy of financial revenues and expenditures of local governments. It cannot be interpreted from a standardized perspective because the systems and policies vary by country. A country that has different historical context and situational characteristics. The institutions and characteristics that shape local finance in Korea are complex. From the economic development system in the 1960 to the recent decentralized state fiscal system, the characteristics of the local finance system vary depending on the stage of national development.

It is not appropriate to interpret local finance in Korea from the Western perspective. Major countries historically formed their modern capitalist state systems with local autonomy. When interpreting the systems and phenomena of self-government and decentralization or local finance, there are many "problematic" areas from the Western perspective, but in the historical context of Korea, they are part of a transition. Interpretation is more important than criticism.

In case of local finance in South Korea, various contexts are interwoven in the process of forming the financial system of self-governing and decentralized local governments, starting from the frontline administrative agencies of the central government. This book describes and characterizes the local finance system in Korea. From the perspective of decentralization, Korean local finance has three distinctive features when compared to major countries.

First, there is the complexity of central-local fiscal relations in the process of transitioning from a centralized system to a self-governing and decentralized system in a developing country. There are many aspects that are not appropriate to interpret only from the perspective of Western financial theory.

Second, the development of local finance is the history of welfare finance since the rise of local government. The issues surrounding local welfare finance are considerable. In the framework of various local finance systems formed in local development governance during the low-income countries, there is a dual nature of the system that needs to carry out social welfare finance projects that support national growth in recent developed countries.

Third, the duality or inconsistency between administrative decentralization and fiscal decentralization is reflected in the local finance system as the central government's fiscal management supervision function over local governments continues to expand in the process of expanding self-government and decentralization.

From the perspective of rational institutional design, it is possible to criticize irrationality and arbitrariness. However, local finance systems are not the domain of logical design. They are the result of historical context and social environment. There are many compatible and conflicting elements in individual schemes. It is not a realm of right and wrong. It is a general phenomenon and product of the development of local governance in developing countries.

This book is the first booklet in Korea that explains and analyzes the system and features of Korean local finance in English. It is written as a introductory book for foreign students who are studying abroad in Korea and selecting majors in the social sciences to systematically learn about the Korean local finance system.

The book consists into nine chapters. Chapter 1 is an overview of the comprehensive nature of local finance. Chapters 2 through 4 describe the local revenue system by revenue source. Chapter 5 describes Local Public Enterprises, and Chapter 6 describes the Local Government Finance Management System. Chapters 7 through 9 summarize representative issue topics in local finance. They are Values Budgeting System, Social Welfare Expenditure, and Fiscal Decentralization.

The importance and role of local finance in Korea's national development process is not well understood. A country does not develop through central government policies alone. The Central and the Local must be balanced as two wheels of the cart to drive national growth. It is expected that the Korean experience and the current local finance system will be useful for developing countries to innovate their fiscal systems.

This book was published by the Korean Society of Local Finance with the support of C&F System. We would like to express our gratitude to CEO Jungsu Park for sponsoring the publication of this book. We would like to thank Jaehoon Jeong, President of Yoon Seong Sa, for his efforts in editing and proofreading. Finally, we would like to thank the members of the Korean Society of Local Finance who participated in the English translation of the technical terms of local finance and the explanation of the local finance system in Korea.

November 2023
All authors

Table of Contents

Preface ··· 4

Chapter 1

Introduction

Section 1 Significance of Local Finance   19

  1. Significance of Local Finance ···································· 19
  2. Local Finance-related Laws ······································ 21
  3. The New Normal Transition and Changing Environment ············ 25

Section 2 Size and Composition of Local Finance   27

  1. National Finance and Local Finance ······························ 27
  2. Local Government Revenue ······································ 31
  3. Local Government Expenditure ·································· 33

Section 3 Key Fiscal Indicators for Local Finance   37

  1. Significance of Key Indicators in Local Finance ···················· 37
  2. Fiscal Independence Index and Fiscal Autonomy Index ············ 37
  3. Fiscal Capacity Index ·· 40

Chapter 2

Local Revenue and Own-Source

Section 1 The System and Status of Local Taxes   41

1. Significance of Local Taxes ·· 41
2. System and Classification of Local Taxes ······································· 43
3. Size and Regional Distribution of Local Taxes ································ 45

Section 2 Issues and Policy Challenges of Local Taxation   49

1. Structure of National Tax-Local Tax Revenue Share ······················ 49
2. Tax Price Principle and Taxation Sovereignty ································ 50
3. Local Tax Non-Local Resources ··· 54

Section 3 Local Non-Tax Revenue   54

1. Significance of Local Non-Tax Revenue ·· 54
2. Categories of Local Non-Tax Revenue ··· 56
3. Current Status of Local Non-Tax Revenue ······································ 58

Chapter 3

Local Revenue and Dependent Financial Resources

Section 1 Local Share Tax   60

1. The Purpose of the Local Share Tax ································60
2. Composition and Funding of the Local Share Tax ····················· 61
3. General Share Tax and Adjustments ·······························65
4. Policy Goals of Local Share Tax System ····························66

Section 2 Adjustment Grant and Regional Coexistent Development Fund   69

1. City & County Adjustment Grant ·································69
2. Autonomous District Adjustment Grants ····························69
3. Regional Coexistent Development Fund ······························71
4. Policy Goals of AG & RCDF ····································· 72

Section 3 Subsidy   75

1. The Purpose of Subsidy ······································· 75
2. National Subsidy Trends ······································ 76
3. The Rates of Subsidies in National Subsidy Projects ···················· 77
4. Balanced Regional Development Special Account ·······················80
5. Policy Agenda in the Subsidy System ······························82

Chapter 4
Local Bond

Section 1 Definition and Types of Local Bonds	86
1. Definition of Local Bonds	86
2. Types of Local Bonds based on the Purposes	87
3. Types of Local Bonds with Bond Issuance Method	89
Section 2 Local Bond Management System	90
1. Management of Local Bonds by MOIS	90
2. Local Bond Management by Local Governments	92
Section 3 Future Tasks for Local Bond Management	93
1. Enhancing the Utilization Strategies of Local Bonds	93
2. Adoption of Specialized Techniques for Management	94
3. Governmental Support by the Central Government	94
4. Establishment of a Specialized Network	95

Chapter 5
Local Fiscal Management System

Section 1 The Purpose of a Fiscal Management System	96
1. Budget Management Process of Local Governments	96
2. Decentralization and Local Fiscal Management	98

Section 2 Pre-Budget System — 100

1. The Mid-term Local Finance Plan ··100
2. Feasibility Study and Local Financial Impact Assessment ············101
3. Local Finance Investment Review ·······································101

Section 3 Post-Fiscal Management — 103

1. Local Finance Analysis System ··103
2. Financial Crisis Management ··104

Section 4 Subsidy and Local Fiscal Management — 105

1. Political Economy of Subsidies ··105
2. Management of National Subsidies by MOIS ·························106
3. Evaluation of Subsidy Project System ··································107

Chapter 6

Local Public Enterprises

Section 1 The Meaning of Local Public Enterprises — 108

1. Significance of Local Public Enterprises ································108
2. Types and Businesses of Local Public Enterprises ····················109

Section 2 Financial Situations of Local Public Enterprises — 111

1. Financial Scale of Local Public Enterprises ····························111
2. Financial Soundness of the Local Public Enterprises ················114
3. Political Economy of Debt and Public Fees ····························116

Section 3 Management of Local Public Enterprises ... 118

1. Local Public Enterprises Management Evaluation ... 118
2. Management Innovation Issues ... 118

Chapter 7

Value Budgeting and Financial Management

Section 1 Participatory Budgeting ... 121

1. Significance of Participatory Budgeting ... 121
2. Introduction of Participatory Budgeting ... 122
3. Issues of Participatory Budgeting ... 122

Section 2 Local Government Gender Budget System ... 124

1. Significance of the Gender Budget System ... 124
2. Main Contents of the Gender Budget Statement ... 125
3. Issues of the Gender Budget System ... 127

Section 3 Local Grant Budget Management ... 128

1. Significance of Local Grant ... 128
2. Local Grant Budget and Management ... 129
3. Issues in Managing the Local Grant Budget ... 129

Chapter 8

Social Welfare and Local Finance

Section 1 Welfare Decentralization and Local Finance　　131

1. Local Finance and Social Welfare Expenditure ································· 131
2. Local Finance as the Main Player in Welfare Policy ························ 132
3. Welfare Decentralization and Local Finance ································· 134

Section 2 Issues of Local Social Welfare Expenditure　　136

1. Status of Welfare Expenditure in Local Finance ······························ 136
2. Issues in and Inter-Governmental Welfare Finance ························· 139

Section 3 Reform Tasks for Welfare Finance　　143

1. Guaranteeing Local General Revenue ·· 143
2. Reorganization of the Standard Subsidy Rate ································ 144
3. Establishment of the Next-Generation System ································ 145

Chapter 9

Fiscal Decentralization and Intergovernmental Relations

Section 1 Significance of Fiscal Decentralization　　148

1. Meaning of Decentralization and Fiscal Decentralization ················ 148
2. Three Theoris about Fiscal Decentralization ·································· 149
3. Own-Sourcism and General Resourcism ······································· 152

4. History of Fiscal Decentralization ································ 153

Section 2 Decentralization Share Tax   155

1. Significance of the Decentralization Share Tax System ···················· 155
2. Funding and Allocation Method for DST ···························· 157
3. Key Issues Regarding the DST ····································· 158

Section 3 Balanced Regional Development Special Account(BRD-SA)
                                                                    160

1. Significance of the BRD-SA ······································ 160
2. Operational Framework ·· 162
3. Implications of the BRD-SA and Fiscal Decentralization ················ 163

Section 4 The Transfer of National Tax to Local Tax   167

1. The Moon Jae-in Administration's Decentralization Initiative ············· 167
2. Two-Stage Fiscal Decentralization ································· 167
3. Characteristics and Policy Implications ···························· 169

References ·· 172
Index ··· 176

Korean Local Finance

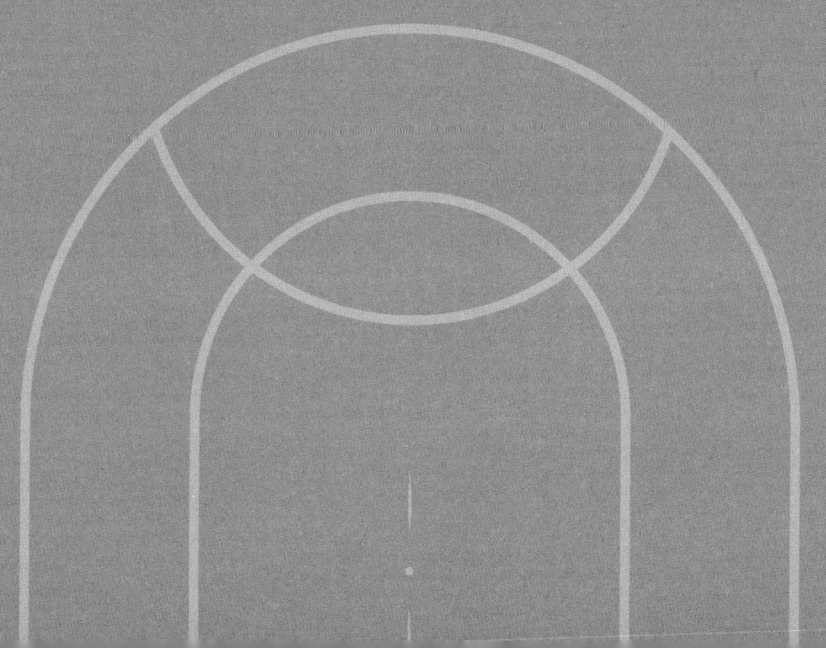

Chapter 1

Introduction

Section 1 Significance of Local Finance

1. Significance of Local Finance

The Field of Practical Guideline & Social Value

Local Finance encompasses the revenue generation and financial expenditure functions of local governments, as well as the supervision and management of local finances by the central government. The study of Local Finance, which explains and interprets the phenomena of local finance, is not only a practical guideline but also an academic discipline that contributes to local self-government and decentralization.

"Local" carries the meaning of a specific location or place. The primary theme in interpreting "local" is "diversity and discretion." Behind diversity lies the issue of "disparity." Interpretations of disparity and diversity are within the realm of values. When interpreting locality based on national standards, there can be issues of excess and deficiency institutionally. Therefore, locality is within the context of concepts like "Self-Government and Decentralization." In contrast, the primary theme of "finance" is "standard, rigor, transparency." Local finance is a policy area that balances diversity in the region and rigor in finance.

Local Revenue

Local revenue refers to the money that a local government secures within a fiscal year. Taxes paid by citizens to the state are allocated between the central government and local governments according to legal regulations and fiscal functions. A considerable portion of the tax revenues allocated to the central government is transferred to local governments through the finance adjustment system.

The central government sustains its operations with the taxes collected from citizens. Although there are other sources of income apart from taxes, such as national facility entrance fees or the sale of national land, the majority of funding is obtained through national tax collected by the National Tax Service. In contrast, local government's funding sources are diverse. Some come from local taxes paid by citizens to the local government, while others are funds transferred from the central government.

Local Expenditure

Local expenditure refers to the expenses incurred by a local government within a fiscal year. One of the key distinctions from the central government's expenditure is that it is limited to spending within the jurisdiction. Consequently, within local expenditure, efficiency issues related to geographical externalities and economies of scale in public services arise. There are also responsibility issues regarding the residents within the jurisdiction who should bear the responsibility for these expenditures.

Local Finance Management

In a unitary system country with a national-local government political system, the central government holds strong oversight and management functions over the financial activities of local governments. Various financial systems related to this are collectively referred to as the local government finance management system. A notable example is the Budgeting Guideline issued by the Ministry of Interior and Safety, which provides guidance to local governments. Additionally, there are systems such as the Fiscal Investment Review System, Mid-Term Local Finance Plan, and Financial Crisis Management System.

The Ministry of Economy and Finance oversees the allocation of funds for national subsidies and intervenes in local government finances through the management of funds related to the Balanced Regional Development Special Account. Various central government ministries like the Ministry of Health and Welfare establish financial relationships between the central and local governments, often centered around different forms of national subsidy programs.

2. Local Finance-related Laws

Constitution

The Constitution is the highest legal norm that defines the identity of a country. While the current Constitution does not have specific clauses related to local finance, one can deduce the constitutional position of local finance from clauses related to local autonomy. There are two clauses in Chapter 8 of the Constitution, which deals with local autonomy, that provide a basis for this interpretation. These clauses pertain to the general implementation of local autonomy, rather than specific regulations regarding "decentralization" or the value of self-governance in local finance.

The Constitution does not contain provisions for the "central government" and "local government" but assumes the relationship between the national and local government in a unitary system country. The types of local government are determined by the national government through the Local Autonomy Act. Under the Local Autonomy Act, the nature of local government is considered as a "corporation." Therefore, it is not a form of government that divides the sovereignty of the state between the central and local levels. Based on these comprehensive intergovernmental relations regulations, the central government can directly or indirectly intervene in all matters at the local level, and the scope and intensity of local government's autonomy are confined within the purview of central government laws.

> **(Current Constitution) Chapter 8: Local Autonomy**
>
> Article 117
> ① Local Governments handle affairs related to the welfare of residents, manage property, and can establish regulations concerning self-governance within the scope of the law.
> ② The types of Local Governments are determined by law.
>
> Article 118
> ① Local Governments have councils.
> ② The organization, authority, election of council members, the appointment method of the head of the Local Government, and other matters related to the organization and operation of Local Governments are determined by law.

The Local Autonomy Act and the Local Finance Act

The fundamental legal basis for the financial operation principles and revenue sources of local governments can be found in Chapter 7 of the Local Autonomy Act. It regulates the relationship between national finances and Local Finance, as well as principles governing Local Government's revenue and budget operations. Article 122 of the Local Autonomy Act specifies "sound financial operation" for local finance. Because the principle of fiscal balance is prescribed when operating local finance, raising funds through debt instruments like local bonds in local expenditures is difficult to prioritize. The Local Autonomy

Act specifies a finance principle centered on the nation. Article 123 stipulates that "local governments must strive to achieve national policies."

The Local Finance Act has the character of a "basic law" concerning the financial operation and management of local governments. However, despite its symbolic name, it does not have a high legal status, and Article 145 of the Local Autonomy Act states that "matters necessary for local government finance other than those provided in this law shall be separately specified by law." It is, therefore, a general law established in accordance with this provision. The purpose of the Local Finance Act is to establish the basic principles of local government finance to ensure the sound and transparent operation of local finance and autonomy(Local Finance Act Article 1). Accordingly, the fundamental values of Local Finance operation can be summarized as soundness, transparency, and autonomy.

The Local Finance Act contains specific provisions regarding Local Government's financial operation. It includes legal provisions related to the Local Budgeting Guideline, Mid-Term Local Finance Plan, Local Fiscal Investment Review System, Local Finance Analysis and Diagnosis System, Financial Crisis Management System, Adjustment Grant System, National Subsidy Management System, Participatory Budgeting System, Gender Budget System, and other such systems.

Local Revenue-Related Legislation

Local government's revenue consists of local tax, non-tax revenue, local share tax, adjustment grant, subsidies, and local bonds. Among these, local tax and local share tax are regulated by separate laws. The regulations related to the adjustment grant system and local bonds can be found in the Local Finance Act, while regulations related to subsidies can be found in both the Local Finance Act(Ministry of Interior and Safety) and the Subsidy Management Act(Ministry of Economy and Finance).

The primary legal basis for local government's own revenue, which is Local Tax, includes three key laws: the Framework Act on Local Taxes, the Local Tax Act, and the Act On Restriction On Special Cases Concerning Local Taxation. The "Framework Act on Local Taxes" specifies basic matters related to local tax and the rights, obligations, and remedies for taxpayers. The "Local Tax Act" outlines the conditions and procedures for the assessment and collection of all local taxes imposed by local governments. Unlike national tax, which has separate independent laws for each tax category, Local Tax is regulated by a single law, the Local Tax Act.

The Local Share Tax law regulates the funding, purposes of operation, and distribution methods of local share tax, which is a major source of revenue for local government. This law, enacted in 1961, has undergone several revisions over the years. The primary objective of the Local Share Tax law, as stated in Article 1, is to provide Local Government with the necessary funding for administrative operations and fiscal adjustment.

The legal basis for central government subsidies for "projects" managed by various ministries and agencies is managed separately by each central government ministry. However, the integrated management of central government "subsidies" is regulated by the "Subsidy Management Act," which is operated by the Ministry of Economy and Finance. The standard subsidy rate for each central government subsidy project is specified in the "Enforcement Decree of the Subsidy Management Act, Table1." Not all central government subsidy programs are covered in this table. In exceptional cases, such as the Basic Pension program operated by the Ministry of Health and Welfare, the Standard Subsidy Rate is specified in the Basic Pension Act.

Local Public Enterprises Act

The Local Public Enterprises Act was established in 1969. It is a law designed to regulate matters necessary for the operation of enterprises that local government directly establishes, operates, or sets up as legal entities to rationalize their management. The legal basis for public institutions under the central government varies. Some have independent laws, while others are specified as separate chapters within individual business-related laws, and in some cases, they are regulated within a single provision. In contrast, local public enterprises are managed as a whole through a single provision in the law.

Various Related Laws for Local Finance Practical Support

To ensure transparency in the accounting and efficient management of funds for Local Government, the "Local Accounting Act" was established in 2016. This law encompasses principles and standards for accounting, as well as regulations on financial statements, revenue and expenditure, and the duties of accounting public officials.

For the management and operation of funds established by Local Government, there is the "Local Government Fund Management Basic Act." The "Act on Contracts Involving Local Government" sets forth principles, standards, and procedures for various contracts executed by local government.

Legal provisions concerning the protection, acquisition, maintenance, preservation, operation, and disposal of public property and commodities owned by Local Government can be found in the "Public Property And Commodity Management Act."

3. The New Normal Transition and Changing Environment

In the context of comprehensive intergovernmental relations between the central government and local government, the characteristics of local finance have historically been associated with a standardized vertical hierarchy. A vertical financial operation and management system has been established through the standardization of three layers: central, regional, and local. However, this past system has faced challenges due to five significant changes in the new normal environment.

First, the trend towards self-government and decentralization has expanded into discussions about the need for a "Decentralized State," requiring a transformation of the vertical relationship between the national and local governments into a more horizontal one in the event of constitutional amendments for decentralization. Based on this shift, structural changes are expected in the distribution of tax revenues between governments and the central government's management of local finance functions. This expansion would encompass areas such as Educational Autonomy and Police Autonomy, significantly enlarging the administrative and financial domains of local government.

Second, the legal forms of local government have expanded beyond standardized municipalities and counties to include areas designated as "special" or "exceptional." Examples include the transition of Jeju and Gangwon to special self-governing provinces, the redesignation of cities with populations exceeding one million as special cities, and the emergence of Megalopolis Alliances such as the Special Local Government of Busan, Ulsan, and Gyeongnam. As the legal structure of Local Government undergoes changes, discussions about reforming Local Finance are also underway.

Third, the diverse demographic characteristics among local governments have given rise to disparities and crises, with fiscal gaps deepening between metropolitan area and noncapital region local governments, making fiscal balance recovery challenging. Concerns about "local extinction" have led to the official designation of depopulation areas, triggering discussions on revising the methods and content of financial support for these regions.

Fourth, local Finance is legally defined as financial activities within the administrative jurisdiction. However, the geographical diversity of residents' socioeconomic activities in modern society has led to inefficiencies and fiscal blind spots due to the monopoly of jurisdiction in the production and supply of local public services. The institutionalized geographical conditions of Local Finance no longer align with the geographical conditions of citizens' daily lives in many areas.

Fifth, the composition criteria for the "population," which forms the basis for local finance adjustment and revenue distribution, are changing. local finance is based on the registered population living within the jurisdiction of local government. Changes in demographics, such as the separation of workplace and residence and the diversity of lifestyles, have resulted in differences between registered population and the actual living population. The Ministry of Interior and Safety is exploring ways to directly incorporate the "living population"(e. g., temporary residents, tourists) who use public services in a local government without registering their address into the Local Finance Adjustment System.

Section 2 Size and Composition of Local Finance

1. National Finance and Local Finance

Comparison of Budget and Expenditure Standards between Governments

Understanding and interpreting the size of financial resources between the central and local governments, as well as the distribution of responsibilities for budgeting and expenditure based on the tax revenues collected from citizens, is essential. In recent years, the share of local finance in national finances has been steadily increasing, making issues related to the efficiency and accountability of fiscal expenditure more critical.

As of the 2023 original budget net amount, the total budget size for the entire nation is 887.2 trillion won, with the central government accounting for more than half, at 54.6%. This figure is based on revenue standards. In terms of expenditure, the total expenditure amount, excluding overlapping expenditures between the central and local governments, is 652.2 trillion won. The expenditure size of local government is 297.0 trillion won, making up 45.5% of the total, which is larger than the central government's 39.1%.

<Table 1-1> Sizes of Central Government, Local Government, and Local Education Authority Budgets

(based on budget size) (Unit: billion won, %)

	2010	2015	2020	2023
Central Government	2,259,413 (55.5)	2,862,938 (55.7)	3,862,379 (54.1)	4,843,752 (54.6)
Local Government	1,398,565 (34.4)	1,732,590 (33.7)	2,532,263 (35.5)	3,054,109 (34.4)
Local Educational Special Account	410,954 (10.1)	543,341 (10.6)	739,013 (10.4)	974,192 (11.0)

(based on total financial use)

	2010	2015	2020	2023
Central Government	1,362,357 (43.7)	1,669,023 (42.5)	2,163,914 (40.7)	2,549,290 (39.1)
Local Government	1,335,584 (42.8)	1,694,587 (43.2)	2,396,034 (45.0)	2,970,204 (45.5)
Local Educational Special Account	421,205 (13.5)	563,503 (14.3)	761,310 (14.3)	1,002,879 (15.4)

Note: Based on the General Accounts + Special Accounts Original Budget Net Amount
Source: Ministry of Interior and Safety(Each Year), *Local Government Integrated Finance Overview(Part I)*.

The discussions around the decentralized state local finance system primarily focus on minimizing the disparities between the central and local governments in terms of budget size and reducing the fiscal gaps among various government bodies in terms of the total budget expenditure. While the budget size criterion still emphasizes the significance of the central government's financial allocation, in terms of expenditure, Local Finance has gone beyond the realm of central finances.

If we solely consider the numerical scale, we can argue that fiscal decentralization has achieved success. However, "decentralization" is not just a quantitative concept but also a qualitative one. If a significant portion of local finance's expenditures is obligated to follow the central government's directives regarding national affairs, then we should interpret this as an intensified centralization characteristic in terms of expenditure.

Comparison of Regional Share in Local Finance

The distribution of local finance shares by region is similar to the population distribution. Seoul Metropolitan City and Local Metropolitan Cities have significantly larger financial scales. Although there are only seven of them, these metropolitan cities are home to 42.9% of the national population. The portion of Seoul Metropolitan City and the local revenue of the six metropolitan cities' Main Offices and Autonomous Districts account for 36.7% of the total local revenue.

The region with the largest financial scale is Gyeonggi Province, with a budget size of 58.2 trillion won in 2023. Seoul follows with 47.8 trillion won, making it the second-largest in terms of financial scale. The combined financial scale of the Capital Areas (Seoul, Gyeonggi, and Incheon) amounts to 121.5 trillion won, representing 39.8% of the total national local revenue. Although the administrative area of the Capital Area accounts for only 11.8%, it holds a population share of over 50.5%, which is more than half of the national population. The local tax share of Capital Area municipalities exceeds half the national total at 55.0%.

<Table 1-2> Distribution of Local Revenue Share by Region(2023)

(Unit: billion won, person, km²)

	Size			Ratio		
	Revenue	Population	Administrative District area	Revenue	Population	Administrative District area
Seoul	478,118	9,424,873	605	15.7	18.3	0.6
Busan	168,130	3,316,107	771	5.5	6.4	0.8
Daegu	116,282	2,362,880	885	3.8	4.6	0.9
Incheon	155,335	2,969,502	1,067	5.1	5.8	1.1
Gwangju	75,522	1,429,816	501	2.5	2.8	0.5
Daejeon	70,465	1,445,806	540	2.3	2.8	0.5
Ulsan	56,447	1,110,074	1,063	1.8	2.2	1.1
Sejong	18,932	384,496	465	0.6	0.7	0.5
Gyeonggi	581,975	13,596,091	10,200	19.1	26.4	10.2
Gangwon	149,128	1,535,373	16,830	4.9	3.0	16.8
Chungbuk	120,501	1,594,459	7,407	3.9	3.1	7.4
Chungnam	166,242	2,122,913	8,247	5.4	4.1	8.2
Jeonbuk	161,488	1,768,229	8,073	5.3	3.4	8.0
Jeonnam	195,450	1,816,707	12,361	6.4	3.5	12.3
Gyeongbuk	241,723	2,597,527	19,036	7.9	5.1	19.0
Gyeongnam	231,355	3,277,672	10,542	7.6	6.4	10.5
Jeju	67,015	677,493	1,850	2.2	1.3	1.8
Total	3,054,108	51,430,018	100,444	100.0	100.0	100.0

Note: General + Special Accounts Original Budget Net Amount
Source: Ministry of Interior and Safety(2022), *Local Government Integrated Finance Overview(Part 1)*, Statistics Korea National Statistical Portal.

As evident from these indicators, the fiscal disparities and conflicts between the Capital Area and Noncapital Region persist as critical issues.

Due to the distribution characteristics of financial scale, structural issues are latent in local finance policy. These issues revolve around the structural disparities in financial scale, fiscal decentralization, and the efficiency and accountability of fiscal expenditures based on the characteristics of local governments. Simultaneously addressing fiscal imbalances and regional disparities is challenging, particularly concerning the fiscal gap between the Capital Area and Noncapital Region. Strengthening regional development and fiscal equity adjustments by the central government is a complex issue that is not easily resolved in practice.

2. Local Government Revenue

Composition of Local Revenue

There are six sources of revenue for local governments. These include Local Tax, Non-Tax Revenue, Adjustment Grant, Local Share Tax, Subsidies, and Local Bonds. In 2023, based on the original budget gross amount, the most significant source of revenue in the General Accounts revenue category is subsidies, accounting for 39.7%. Following that, Local tax accounts for 32.0%, and Local Share Tax for 17.2%.

Local Tax and Non-Tax Revenue represent the own-source revenue for local governments. Local Share Tax, on the other hand, is a dependent financial resource, transferring 19.24% of Internal Tax from the central government's national tax to local finance. Except for some funds included in the Local Share Tax, most of its revenue is considered General Resources without designated expenditure purposes.

<Table 1-3> Composition of General Accounts Revenue by Local Government Type(2023)

(Unit: %, billion won)

		Local Tax	Non-Tax Revenue	Local Share Tax	Adjustment Grant	Subsidy	Local Bond	Revenue from Carry-Over and Others Internal Trading	Total	(Size)
Regional Governments	Seoul	74.3	3.9	0.6	-	18.9	0.0	2.3	100.0	334,661
	Metropolitan Cities	43.0	2.2	14.7	-	33.8	1.0	5.2	100.0	456,762
	Sejong	54.6	3.9	6.1	-	22.2	0.1	13.1	100.0	15,959
	Provinces	38.5	1.2	9.7	-	48.1	0.1	2.3	100.0	892,609
	Jeju	31.9	3.1	35.9	-	24.5	1.2	3.5	100.0	58,731
Basic Local Governments	Cities	23.8	4.4	23.9	5.9	37.6	0.2	4.2	100.0	956,031
	Counties	8.5	3.3	45.2	3.2	35.0	0.0	4.8	100.0	459,138
	Districts	18.3	5.9	3.0	13.0	54.9	0.0	4.8	100.0	486,914
Total		32.0	3.3	17.2	3.7	39.7	0.2	3.9	100.0	3,660,805
Size(in billion won)		1,172,115	122,251	628,645	134,774	1,452,914	8,231	141,875	3,660,805	

Note: Based on General Accounts Original Budget
Source: Ministry of Interior and Safety(2022). *Integrated Financial Overview of Local Government(Part 1)*.

Composition of Local Revenue by Local Government Type

The composition of local revenue varies by the type of local government. In Seoul Metropolitan City and Metropolitan Cities, local tax accounts for the highest proportion of revenue. In the case of Seoul, the local tax share is significant at 74.3%. In contrast, for provinces and autonomous districts, subsidies have the highest share. In the case of counties, the Local Share Tax accounts for a substantial 45.2% of revenue, while local tax only makes up 8.5%.

Autonomous districts do not receive the General Share Tax from the Local Share Tax. Instead, they receive the Adjustment Grant from the Seoul & metropolitan city. The Autonomous District Adjustment Grant legally defines a certain percentage of the ordinary tax within local tax through an ordinance and operates similarly to the Local Share Tax.

City and counties, which are local governments, receive the City/County Adjustment Grant from the province. The subcategories of Local Share Tax, such as Special Share Tax and Real Estate Share Tax, are also provided to autonomous districts.

3. Local Government Expenditure

Division of Fiscal Functions between Central and Local

In the theory of intergovernmental fiscal relations, the core function of Local Finance is to provide services for the daily lives of residents. However, in reality, the role of Local Government is diverse. Institutionally, Local Government acts both as the autonomous unit of residents and as an executing agency of the central government. On one hand, it uses revenue collected from local residents to carry out its Inherent Affairs, and on the other hand, it utilizes subsidy funds to execute various tasks delegated by the central and upper-level governments.

While there is a theoretical distinction between Local Government's Inherent Affairs and Agency Delegated Affairs, it is not always easy to make a clear-cut distinction in practice. Given the many changes in the fiscal functions and the administrative environment surrounding local government, it is difficult to establish a convincing separation between central, local, and local government-level tasks. Therefore, considering the examples specified in the Local Autonomy Act for local government affairs is a more appropriate approach, despite its arbitrary nature.

Comparison of Fiscal Functions between the Central and Local

By comparing the expenditure functions of the central government and local government, we can understand the characteristics of intergovernmental fiscal functions. In 2023, based on the original budget net amount, the central government's general accounts budget is 446.2 trillion won, while local government's general and special accounts budget is 305.4 trillion won.

In terms of expenditure functions, both the central and local governments exceed 20% in General Public Administration(including personnel expenses and operating expenses). Excluding this category, several characteristics of fiscal functions between the central and local governments can be observed:

First, expenditures related to unification, diplomacy, national defense, and communication are exclusively handled by the central government. These are typical expenditures related to national public services.

Second, both the central and local governments allocate significantly more funds to social affairs than to economic development. In the case of the central government, the budget allocation for economic development in 2023 is 11.5%, while social development accounts for 45.3%. As the country transitions from the state-led economic development era of the 1960s to the welfare state era of the 21st century, government spending on social welfare has been consistently increasing.

Third, expenditures in the field of social welfare represent a significant share of both central and local government budgets. However, 89.6% of local government's welfare spending is for supplementary programs. In local finance, Social Services Expenditures are carried out through a "delegated" system, where local government executes nationwide projects designed by the central government. Considering that the share of basic welfare spending, such as Livelihood Benefit, Medical Benefits, and Basic Pension, is significantly high, there is a characteristic of mandatory mobilization of local resources for central-purpose Basic Welfare Programs.

Fourth, in Environmental Protection Costs, the central government's expenditure is 5.7 trillion won, while local government's expenditure is 29.3 trillion won, which is 5.1 times higher. In Local Finance, 56.9% of Environmental Protection Costs are own-source projects. However, environmental policies are subject to nationwide standardized regulations. Therefore, the central government's role is more focused on legislating various environmental regulations and encouraging local government to carry out own-source projects, rather than direct fiscal expenditure.

Fifth, in the field of regional development within local finance, the emphasis on transportation and land development costs is relatively high. These expenditure sectors have a high proportion of own-source projects, and there is weak fiscal control by the central government, giving local governments significant discretion over spending. As a result, local governments tend to prioritize financial expenditure in the regional development sector, possibly due to the socio-economic characteristics of the projects and the simultaneous operation of local autonomy in project planning and execution.

<Table 1-4> Allocation of Functions between Central and Local Expenditure(2023)

(Unit: %, billion won)

Category	Subcategory	Central Government	Local Governments Total (Sectors)	Local Governments Total (Expenses)	Policy Projects Subsidy project	Policy Projects Own-source Projects	Administrative Operating Expenses	Financial Activities
General Administration	General Public Administration	23.7	5.4	100.0	7.2	73.4	0.0	19.5
	Public Order and Safety	4.7	1.9	100.0	32.5	48.6	0.0	18.9
Unification Diplomacy	Unified Diplomacy	0.8	-	-	-	-	-	-
National Defense	National Defense	12.9	-	-	-	-	-	-
	Subtotal	42.1	7.4	100.0	13.8	66.9	0.0	19.3
Social Development	Education	21.7	5.3	100.0	4.3	95.1	0.0	0.6
	Culture and Tourism	1.0	4.7	100.0	38.0	60.0	0.0	2.0
	Environmental Protection	1.3	9.6	100.0	39.9	56.9	0.0	3.1
	Social Welfare	17.6	31.5	100.0	89.6	9.7	0.0	0.8
	Health	3.6	1.8	100.0	72.6	27.2	0.0	0.2
	Subtotal	45.3	52.9	100.0	66.9	31.8	0.0	1.3
Economic (Regional) Development	Agriculture, Forestry, Marine, and Fisheries	2.0	6.7	100.0	66.7	32.3	0.0	1.0
	industry-small and medium-sized businesses	2.5	2.7	100.0	40.2	53.6	0.0	6.2
	Transportation	3.2	8.1	100.0	27.2	65.0	0.0	7.8
	Communication	0.2	-	-	-	-	-	-
	Land and Regional Development	1.7	5.6	100.0	28.9	60.8	0.0	10.2
	Science and Technology	1.8	0.1	100.0	26.1	72.6	0.0	1.3
	Subtotal	11.5	23.2	100.0	40.5	53.3	0.0	6.2
Other	Reserve fund	1.0	16.6	100.0	0.1	22.5	76.7	0.7
	Total	100.0	100.0	100.0	45.8	37.9	12.7	3.6
	(Size)	4,462,420	3,054,107		1,398,191	1,156,102	388,473	111,341

Note: The central government follows the General Accounts, while local governments follow the General Accounts + Special Accounts Original Budget Net Amount basis.
Source: Ministry of Interior and Safety(2023), 2023 Local Government Integrated Finance Overview(Part 1), Ministry of Economy and Finance(2023), 2023 Summary of Budget.

Section 3 Key Fiscal Indicators for Local Finance

1. Significance of Key Indicators in Local Finance

In local finance, various political and policy values such as Self-government and decentralization, efficiency, soundness, and accountability are embedded. The Ministry of Interior and Safety and local governments establish and use key indicators symbolizing local finance's status, which include Fiscal Independence Index and Fiscal Autonomy Index. These indicators are used primarily when explaining local finance conditions and operating the local finance adjustment system by various central government agencies.

Fiscal Independence Index and Fiscal Autonomy Index, along with other key indicators in local finance, are related to intergovernmental fiscal relations. These indicators are primarily used by various central government agencies, including the Ministry of Interior and Safety, to explain the conditions of local finance and operate the local finance adjustment system. They serve as top-priority policy indicators in local finance.

While the challenges of Self-government and decentralization remain important in the current era, local finance's representative indicators are also crucial numerical data used as a foundation for various policy tasks. This includes tasks related to efficiency, accountability, and fairness, even in a local finance system that has grown alongside central finances at an equal level.

2. Fiscal Independence Index and Fiscal Autonomy Index

Fiscal Independence Index
The Fiscal Independence Index is a fiscal indicator that calculates the proportion of own-source in local revenue and expresses it as a ratio. It serves as a symbol of Self-government and decentralization and was used as a key indicator for explaining the situation of local finance until the

early 2000s. During the Fifth Republic's Chun Doo-hwan government, the Fiscal Independence Index was employed as a political tool to avoid implementing local autonomy. Article 10 of the Supplementary Provisions of the Fifth Republic Constitution stated, "local councils under this Constitution shall be established sequentially, taking into account the Fiscal Independence Index of Local Government, and the timing of such establishment shall be determined by law."

This index embodies the values of revitalizing local autonomy for democratization and measures the degree of Self-government and decentralization in local revenue.

However, as a policy indicator for adjusting financial pressure, fiscal health, regional disparities, and fairness, it has limitations. For example, if the central government expands its financial role in areas facing population decline, the Fiscal Independence Index of the affected local government may decrease, leading to negative criticism. This creates a contradiction where the central government's financial role is limited.

Fiscal Autonomy Index

The Fiscal Autonomy Index is calculated based on the combined revenue of Local Tax, Non-Tax Revenue, Adjustment Grant, and Local Share Tax. It represents the proportion of "General Resource" in the total revenue. The Fiscal Autonomy Index is used as a standard indicator in areas such as Basic Livelihood Security Benefits and Childcare Support Charges, where a Differential Subsidy Ratio is applied for welfare subsidies.

This index has been utilized as a key indicator in local finance since the early 2000s when fiscal decentralization, centered around Local Share Tax, was promoted. In 2005, measures were taken to secure funding through the Decentralization Share Tax for the local transfer of 149 national subsidized projects. This caused the Fiscal Independence Index of local governments to decrease since the dependent financial resources ratio increased due to the inclusion of decentralization share tax as a subcategory of Local Share Tax.

<Table 1-5> Fiscal Independence Index and Fiscal Autonomy Index by Local Government Type(2023)

	Seoul	Metro-politan Cities	Sejong	Provinces	Jeju	Cities	Counties	Districts	All regions
Fiscal Independence Index(A)	77.0	43.7	57.2	36.7	51.9	33.3	28.2	11.8	24.2
Fiscal Autonomy Index(B)	77.6	58.7	63.5	48.6	52.6	70.1	58.0	60.2	40.3
Difference (B-A)	0.6	15.0	6.3	11.9	0.7	36.8	29.8	48.4	16.1

Note: Based on General Accounts Original Budget
Source: Ministry of Interior and Safety(2023). *Integrated Financial Overview of Local Government(Part 1).*

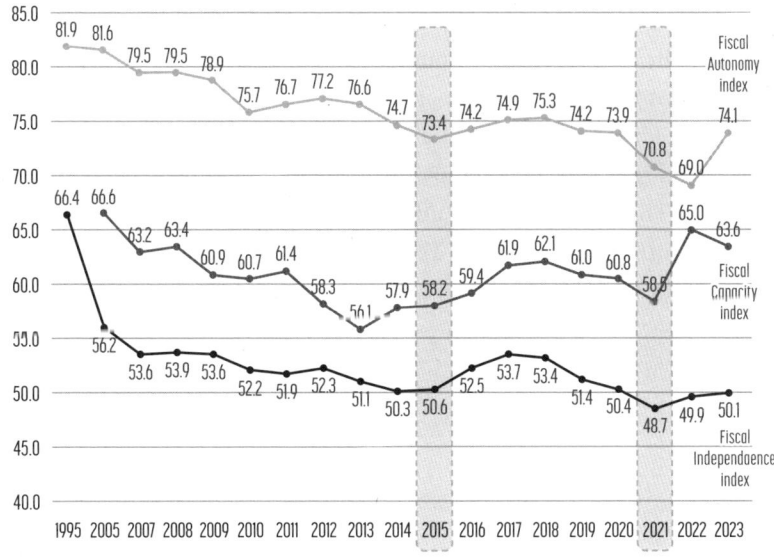

[Figure 1-1] Trends in the Fiscal Independence Index and Fiscal Autonomy Index Over the Years

Note: Based on the General Accounts Original Budget
Source: Local Finance365 www.lofin.mois.go.kr

Given this context, the name of the index was changed to "Fiscal Autonomy Index," which includes the ratio of general resources, including Local Share Tax. It was established as a representative indicator in local finance policy. The Fiscal Autonomy Index is characterized as a policy indicator that aims to achieve both "balance-decentralization" in financial terms.

3. Fiscal Capacity Index

Another indicator to assess local revenue capacity is the "Fiscal Capacity Index." The Fiscal Capacity Index serves as a metric for ensuring the "financial support" for local governments. This index is calculated based on the proportion of the standard amount of financial revenue to the Standard Amount of Financial Demand, and it is used as a standard index for distributing General Share Tax.

From the perspective of the central government, the Standard Amount of Financial Demand is essentially the financial functions that local governments should perform, quantified. The Standard Amount of Financial Revenue is the minimum income that a local government can secure for a year. For local governments with a Fiscal Capacity Index exceeding 1, General Share Tax is not distributed. This is because it is considered that they adequately meet the basic financial expenditure demands. The Fiscal Capacity Index is used as a standard index not only for distributing General Share Tax revenue but also for disbursing Real Estate Share Tax and Municipal Adjustment Grant funds.

Chapter 2

Local Revenue and Own-Source

Section 1 The System and Status of Local Taxes

1. Significance of Local Taxes

Taxation and Local Taxes

The taxes paid by citizens are classified into national taxes and local taxes based on the collecting entity. National taxes are collected by the National Tax Service and disbursed by the central government. Local taxes, on the other hand, are the inherent resources collected by local governments. Local taxes form the foundation of local Government Financial Revenue and are a critical policy area for Fiscal decentralization. However, unlike the single relationship between the government and taxpayers(citizens) in the case of national taxes, Local Taxes operate within a considerably complex system and policy environment.

    Local self-governance is in place, but the legal authority of Local government regarding local tax is limited. According to the Principle of No Taxation Without Law, all taxes must be based on laws enacted by the National Assembly. Local councils cannot introduce local tax categories through ordinances. The relevant ministry for South Korea's local tax-related laws is the Ministry of Interior and Safety.

The vulnerability of local government's taxation sovereignty must be interpreted in the context of the history of self-government and decentralization and the societal environment of taxation policies. The societal or policy positioning of local tax is established within the context of the relationship between local self-governance and the central government, as well as the national identity of taxation related to the protection of citizen's rights and tax policies.

Intergovernmental Revenue and Tax Share Relations

While the central government is responsible for local tax-related laws, the authority for tax imposition, collection, and revenue management belongs to local governments. Additionally, in modern society, national taxes and local taxes are intertwined beyond their legal forms. Although the tax collection entities may seem straightforward, fiscal relationships between the central and local governments become complex during the distribution of tax revenues and the taxation expenditure process. For example, the total amount of value-added tax is distributed between national tax(value-added tax, 74.7%) and local tax(local consumption tax, 25.3%). The taxation object for local income tax is essentially the same as national income tax, and the tax base and tax rates are automatically linked between national tax and local income tax.

Among national taxes, 19.24% of internal taxes(income tax, value-added tax, etc.) are transferred to local governments as local share tax revenue. Gross real estate tax serves as the source of real estate share tax. Among local taxes, local education tax is transferred to local educational governments as revenue, and the automobile tax on pro rata motor fuel is spent on fuel subsidies for taxis and freight vehicles.

Therefore, discussions about the characteristics of local tax or policy challenges related to local tax require an understanding of the comprehensive tax system, including both national taxes and local taxes. It is not appropriate to strictly separate national tax and local tax based on institutional nomenclature. Complex intergovernmental fiscal relationships are formed based on the characteristics of fiscal functions performed by the central and local governments and the convenience of tax revenue collection and distribution.

2. System and Classification of Local Taxes

Local taxes are defined in Article 3 of the "Act On The Adjustment Of National And Local Taxes" as follows: "Local governments shall impose independent taxes, including land tax, entertainment and food tax, property tax, automobile tax, horse race tax, acquisition tax, slaughter tax, license tax, and income tax surcharge, corporate tax surcharge, business tax surcharge, and other earmarked taxes." Based on the tax base, local taxes can be classified into income taxation, consumption taxation, property taxation, and other taxes. Local taxes are collected through cities, counties, and districts and are received through separate bank accounts for each local government. Local taxes differ from national taxes in terms of the collecting authority. National taxes are collected by central government agencies such as the National Tax Service and the Korea Customs Service and are deposited into the Bank of Korea's national treasury account.

Local taxes are classified into ordinary taxes and earmarked taxes, totaling 11 tax items. Among the earmarked taxes, the local resource and facility tax is divided into taxation on community resources and taxation on real estate. The revenue from the former is managed separately through a special account. The local education tax is the revenue of local education special accounts and is entirely transferred to local educational governments.

The local tax system varies depending on the relationship between metropolitan and basic governments, such as autonomous districts in metropolitan cities and provinces in regions. Provincial taxes include acquisition tax, registration and license tax, leisure tax, local consumption tax, local resource and facility tax, and local education tax,

[Figure 2-1] Local Tax System by Type of Local Government

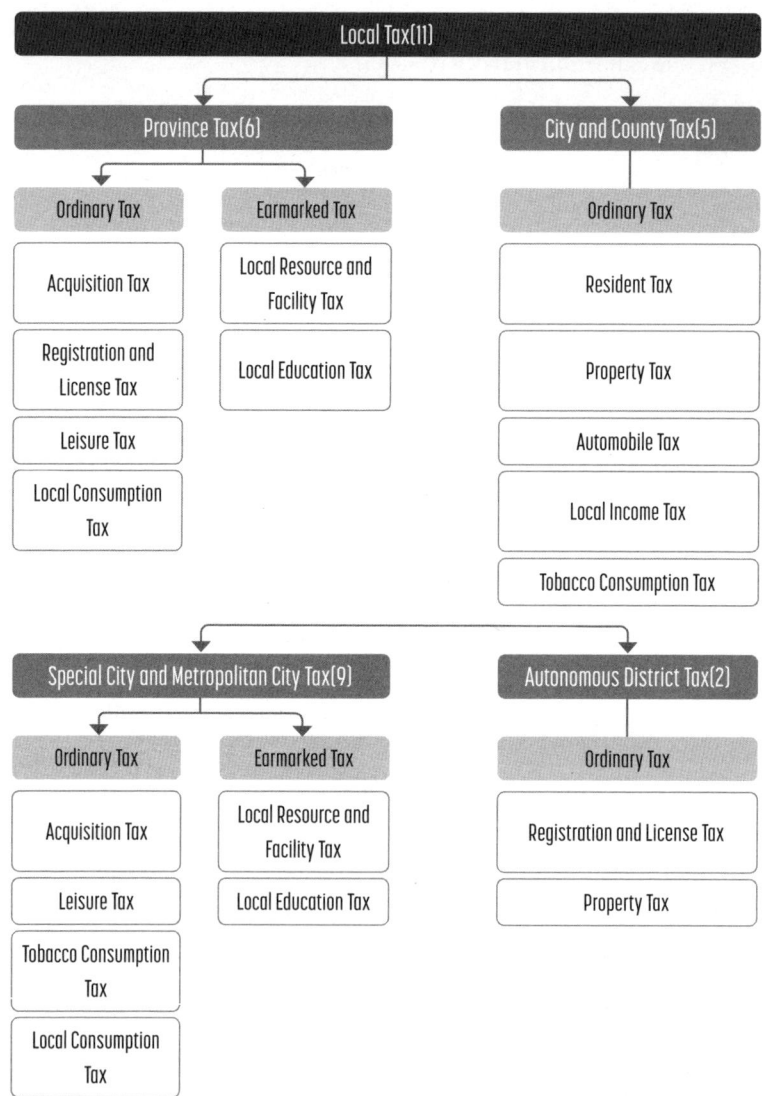

Note: In Seoul, there is joint property tax assessment between the special city and the Autonomous Districts.

while the remaining five tax items are municipal taxes. Autonomous districts have independent local taxes, including only registration and license tax and property tax.

Several tax items are shared between metropolitan and basic governments, leading to differences in the classification of local taxes in the law and tax collection statistics. For example, among local consumption taxes, those related to national transfer(conversion) for local assistance programs are transferred to cities, counties, and districts. Among resident taxes in autonomous districts, taxation on business place and taxation on employees are transferred to autonomous districts. Although the Local Tax Act defines only two local taxes in autonomous districts, the sharing of tax revenues between the main office and local consumption tax and resident tax leads to four tax items in tax statistics.

3. Size and Regional Distribution of Local Taxes

Size of Local Taxes by Category

From the perspective of self-government and decentralization, local taxes are the most important source of revenue for local governments. As of the 2023 original budget net amount, the size of local taxes amounts to 115.3 trillion KRW, accounting for 31.7% of local government revenue. By type of local government, the Local Taxes of Seoul Metropolitan City and the main offices of metropolitan cities amount to 42.45 trillion KRW, representing 36.9% of the total. Regional government offices in metropolitan areas have local taxes totaling 34.3 trillion KRW, which is 29.8% of the total. Of this amount, around half, 16 trillion KRW, comes from the local taxes of the Gyeonggi regional government office. The size and proportion of local taxes for other regional government offices are relatively smaller.

By category, the property transaction taxation, specifically the acquisition tax, amounts to 26.3 trillion KRW, constituting 22.8% of the total, while the property holding tax, known as property tax, amounts

<Table 2-1> Size of Local Taxes by Type of Local Government(2023)

(Unit: %, billion won)

	Metropolitan government				Local Government			Total	Size
	Metropolitan Cities	Sejong	Provinces	Jeju	Cities	Counties	Districts		
Acquisition Tax	26.6	24.4	41.6	26.7				22.8	263,316
Registration and License Tax	0.1	1.4	3.3	1.8			9.4	1.8	20,390
Resident Tax	1.7	1.6		0.8	4.8	3.9	4.5	2.1	23,875
Property Tax	5.2	14.4		11.2	28.0	20.5	77.0	14.4	165,869
Automobile Tax	6.7	6.1		6.0	16.1	18.5		6.4	74,085
Leisure Tax	0.5	0.0	1.7	3.0				0.7	8,635
Tobacco Consumption Tax	3.2	2.0		3.2	7.6	9.1		3.1	35,274
Local Consumption Tax	18.6	30.2	39.0	27.1	6.1	23.0	8.4	21.8	251,276
Local Income Tax	26.8	12.2		10.2	35.9	23.9		18.1	208,131
Local Resource and Facility Tax	1.9	1.7	0.5	1.2	0.1			1.7	19,345
Local Education Tax	8.0	5.8	11.3	7.9				6.5	74,846
Revenue from Previous Year	0.7	0.1	0.1	0.7	1.4	1.2	0.7	0.7	7,602
Total	100.0	100.0	100.0	100.0	100.0	100.0	100.0	100.0	1,152,644
(Size)	425,736	8,720	343,725	18,726	227,347	39,074	89,316	1,152,644	

Note: Based on the Original Budget Net Amount for the year 2023
Source: Ministry of Interior and Safety(2023), 2023 Local Government Integrated Fiscal Overview(Part 1).

to 16.5 trillion KRW, representing 14.4% of the total. Income taxation and consumption taxation also contribute significantly. Notably, local income tax accounts for 18.1%, and local consumption tax is at the 21.8% level. In the past, local tax systems were primarily based on property taxation, but recent efforts have shifted towards a balanced mainstay tax system that includes income, consumption, and property taxes.

Distribution of Local Taxes by Region

The distribution of local tax revenue varies by region, leading to persistent regional imbalances in local finance. When comparing the regional share of tax revenues with 2010, there has been little change. In the case of local taxes, Seoul and Gyeonggi Province have the highest shares at 23.9% and 24.1%, respectively. When including Incheon, the metropolitan area collects over half of the local tax revenue. Consequently, non-capital region municipalities prefer the central government's finance adjustment system over local taxes, as they fear that an emphasis on local taxes could exacerbate the concentration of resources in the metropolitan area.

In recent times, there has been a trend of decreased local tax contribution by the city of Seoul. Seoul argues that, under fiscal pressure, it should receive support from the central government's transfer revenue, such as national subsidy or local share tax, under the same conditions as other local governments. Seoul perceives itself as being at a disadvantage in comparison to other local governments when it comes to transfer finance. If Seoul were to receive more significant transfer revenue from the central government than it currently does, it could potentially trigger a zero-sum game within the national local finance, where the total amount remains fixed.

<Table 2-2> Distribution of Local Taxes by Region

(Unit: billion won, %)

	Size		Proportion		Proportion changes
	2010	2023	2010	2023	
Seoul	134,564	275,835	28.1	23.9	-4.2
Busan	29,313	64,468	6.1	5.6	-0.5
Daegu	19,520	46,374	4.1	4.0	-0.1
Incheon	28,310	60,773	5.9	5.3	-0.6
Gwangju	10,168	26,820	2.1	2.3	0.2
Daejeon	11,034	25,202	2.3	2.2	-0.1
Ulsan	11,592	23,307	2.4	2.0	-0.4
Sejong	-	8,720	-	0.8	-
Gyeonggi	115,506	296,815	24.1	25.8	1.6
Gangwon	11,706	31,087	2.4	2.7	0.3
Chungbuk	11,820	33,417	2.5	2.9	0.4
Chungnam	17,265	49,102	3.6	4.3	0.7
Jeonbuk	11,689	33,062	2.4	2.9	0.4
Jeonnam	11,974	40,586	2.5	3.5	1.0
Gyeongbuk	19,307	51,711	4.0	4.5	0.5
Gyeongnam	30,290	66,620	6.3	5.8	-0.5
Jeju	4,730	18,726	1.0	1.6	0.6
Total	478,788	1,152,644	100.0	100.0	-

Note: Based on the Original Budget Net Amount
Source: Ministry of Interior and Safety(2010; 2023). *Local Government Integrated Fiscal Overview(Part 1).*

Section 2 Issues and Policy Challenges of Local Taxation

1. Structure of National Tax-Local Tax Revenue Share

Tax revenues collected from citizens are distributed between the central government and local governments. Taxes serve the dual purposes of safeguarding the interests of citizens(nation-citizen relationship) and promoting self-government and decentralization (central-local relationship), reflecting their political and economic characteristics. Balancing and regulating power relationships in this context is crucial, as an excessive tilt in either direction is deemed inappropriate. The issue of the revenue share structure between national tax and local tax is consistently raised as a policy challenge in the context of self-government and decentralization. During the Moon Jae-in administration, there was explicit mention of restructuring the national tax-local tax structure to a 7:3 ratio as part of the Presidential agenda.

Local tax revenues, when compared to national tax, have a significantly lower share, maintaining a similar national tax-local tax revenue structure to that of the mid-1990s when local autonomy was revitalized. Back then, the national tax-local tax ratio was 8:2. This ratio symbolized the resurgence of local autonomy but gave rise to a cynical perception that it amounted to only "20% self-governing."

National tax-local tax revenue structures vary among countries. In the UK, national tax predominates, while Japan has a 6:4 structure. Federal nations strive to maintain balance. At the expenditure stage, local finance often exceeds central government fiscal spending, as the central government holds 80% of tax revenues and redistributes them to local governments as transfer revenue. This process leads to inefficiencies and ineffectiveness, including digital divides, moral hazards, and weaknesses in financial performance accountability towards residents.

The disparity between National Tax and Local Tax revenues

decreased in the late 2010s but has recently expanded again. In 2020, with the expansion of local consumption tax, the national tax-local tax revenue share was 73.7:26.3, but by 2023, it had expanded once more to 77.6:22.4. This is primarily due to the relatively high growth rate of national tax revenue and the relative inflexibility of local tax revenue in response to changes in the taxation environment.

The central government operates various national subsidy programs based on its national tax revenue, and when local expenses must be mandatory, the size of the local funding contribution relative to the national revenue increase can become disproportionately large. This is not about the ratio but rather about the scale. In 1991, the difference between national tax and local tax was only 22 trillion won, but by 2023, this gap had grown to more than 285 trillion won, over ten times larger. If local tax revenue is not secured at an appropriate level, it can lead to issues in the central government's fiscal expenditure when running national subsidy programs, including challenges related to funding composition and mobilization.

2. Tax Price Principle and Taxation Sovereignty

Local Tax and Tax Price Principle

In the context of self-government and Decentralization, the principle is that when the central government determines its support for local finance, local government should impose additional financial expenditures on residents through the resolution of the local council. If local government requires more spending or demands public services beyond what is provided by the central government's standard support, it must procure additional funds through local tax by utilizing combinations of taxation objects, tax bases, and tax rates. Connecting the quantity and quality of local public services directly to local tax revenue is known as the Tax Price Principle.

The application of the tax price principle in the current local tax system is limited. Local government's local tax revenue is considered

[Figure 2-2] Trends in National Tax and Local Tax Sizes

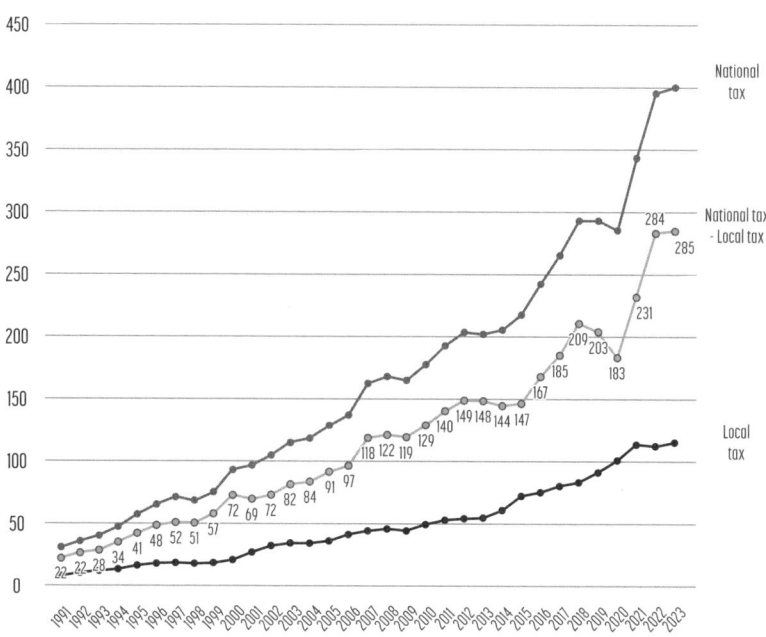

Note: The middle line represents the difference in size between National Tax and Local Tax(e.g., 285 trillion won in 2023).
Source: Ministry of Interior and Safety(Each Year). *Local Government Integrated Fiscal Overview(Part 1)*.

first, and any shortfall is adjusted by the central government through local share tax and national subsidy. It has become a common practice for residents to pay the local tax amount determined by the system, with any additional funding needed post-payment being supplied by the central government through local share tax and national subsidy.

Taxation Sovereignty of Local Government

The reason for the limited activation of the local tax price principle lies in the issue of taxation sovereignty of local government. The authority of local government regarding taxation objects, tax bases, and tax rate determinations within the systems and laws related to local tax is restricted. The central government manages these aspects directly or indirectly, and a standardized local tax system is formed, regardless of the type of local government.

Article 59 of the Constitution explicitly states the "Principle of No Taxation Without Law," emphasizing that taxes can only be imposed through legislation. Local government cannot impose local tax through ordinances. To operate various new revenue sources at the local level as local tax items, there is the local resource and facility tax. However, the validity of new revenue sources must be reviewed by the National Assembly through legislation from a central perspective rather than a regional one. Although the current local tax Act includes elastic tax rates that can be adjusted up to 50%, implementing them at the local level is challenging. Within the current local tax governance structure, elastic tax rates are an ineffectual policy tool.

Local government's substantial authority over mainstay taxes in tax policy is also limited. Property taxation authority is a core policy tool for the central government's real estate policies in the metropolitan area. Local consumption tax and local income tax are linked to national taxes, such as income tax and value-added tax, leaving little room for independent policy-making by local government. In essence, Local Government's autonomy in tax policy is virtually non-existent due to these connections.

Fiscal Adjustment Function of Local Tax

Local tax is considered the inherent resources of local governments, so in principle, there should be no need to consider financial relationships with other local governments. However, the current local tax system includes a finance adjustment system, where the initially collected amount is adjusted and redistributed.

In the case of Seoul Metropolitan City, property tax is operated as a shared tax between autonomous districts and the city main office. Property tax falls under the category of autonomous district taxes, and in Seoul, half of the property tax collected goes to the city main office as property tax revenue. The city main office then distributes equal amounts to the 25 autonomous districts, becoming a source of financial equality for the autonomous districts.

The fiscal adjustment function of local consumption tax is quite complex. The national tax service collects a portion of the total amount of value-added tax, 25.3%, and allocates it as local consumption tax to representative local governments. These funds are distributed based on consumption indexes at the provincial level, applying the principles of taxation on place. Since the distribution share for metropolitan area local governments tends to be excessive, adjustments are made by giving weight to consumption indexes for local metropolitan cities. The metropolitan area is assigned a weight of 100, local metropolitan cities get a weight of 200, while other provinces have a weight of 300. In addition to this, apart from the financial adjustment amount, around one-third of the metropolitan area local consumption tax is temporarily allocated to the coexistent local development fund for ten years, which is shared among local governments nationwide.

Local consumption tax has specific characteristics that distinguish it from regular local taxes, especially since its introduction as a tax category in 2014. It has been endowed with various forms of fiscal adjustment functions, including compensatory adjustments to preserve local tax revenue due to property tax reductions, adjustments due to central government subsidy programs and local transfers, compensatory adjustments for reductions in general share tax, and adjustments for reductions in local education finances.

3. Local Tax Non-Local Resources

As the central government utilizes Local Tax for various policy purposes, the autonomous nature of local government's self-generated revenue is diminishing. Within statistical classifications, certain funds are categorized as local tax, but in reality, local governments have limited autonomy in using these non-local resources. These resources account for a significant portion of local tax but cannot be used autonomously by local governments.

For example, within the local education tax and automobile tax on pro rata motor fuel, the fuel subsidy component cannot be used as a general resource by local governments. The entire local education tax is transferred to a special account for education expenses. Even the preserved portion of the local education tax that increased during the process of reducing the acquisition tax rate in 2013, which was included in the Local Consumption Tax, cannot be directly used by local government.

Considering that the central government specifies the expenditure purposes for these categories, they can be regarded as "earmarked taxes of the central government" that are operated in the form of Local Tax. As of the 2021 fiscal year-end, non-local resources amount to 830 billion won, equivalent to 7.4% of the total local tax revenue.

Section 3 Local Non-Tax Revenue

1. Significance of Local Non-Tax Revenue

As resistance to taxation by taxpayers increases in the mobilization of public resources through taxes, alternative sources of revenue have become important. Non-tax revenue, with user fees as a central component, has gained significance. Non-tax revenue, such as user fees, constitutes direct charges for specific public services, making

<Table 2-3> Size and Proportion of Non-Local Resources within Local Tax

(Unit: billion won, %)

<table>
<tr><th colspan="2"></th><th colspan="2">2014</th><th colspan="2">2021</th></tr>
<tr><th colspan="2"></th><th>Size</th><th>%</th><th>Size</th><th>%</th></tr>
<tr><td colspan="2">Local Education Tax(A)</td><td>56,039</td><td>8.4</td><td>75,890</td><td>6.7</td></tr>
<tr><td colspan="2">Automobile Tax(Pro Rata Motor Fuel, Fuel Tax) (B)</td><td>4,863</td><td>0.7</td><td>4,055</td><td>0.4</td></tr>
<tr><td rowspan="5">Local Consumption Tax (Acquisition Tax Compensation)</td><td>Acquisition Tax, Main</td><td>21,063</td><td>3.2</td><td>31,167</td><td>2.8</td></tr>
<tr><td>Local Education Tax(C)</td><td>2,106</td><td>0.3</td><td>3,117</td><td>0.3</td></tr>
<tr><td>Local Share Tax</td><td>2,065</td><td>0.3</td><td>3,171</td><td>0.3</td></tr>
<tr><td>Transfer Deduction</td><td>204</td><td>0.0</td><td>321</td><td>0.0</td></tr>
<tr><td>Subtotal</td><td>25,438</td><td>3.8</td><td>37,775</td><td>3.3</td></tr>
<tr><td colspan="2">Non-Local Resources(A+B+C)</td><td>63,008</td><td>9.5</td><td>83,062</td><td>7.4</td></tr>
<tr><td colspan="2">Note(local tax amount)</td><td>663,284</td><td>100.0</td><td>1,127,984</td><td>100.0</td></tr>
</table>

Note: 1) Based on settlement of accounts
2) Percentage is the percentage of local tax
Source: Ministry of Interior and Safety(2015; 2022). *Local Tax Statistical Yearbook.*

it particularly important from the perspective of local finance management.

Non-tax revenue comprises all own-source revenues except for taxes and national bonds. It is categorized into national non-tax revenue and local non-tax revenue based on the attributing authority. Since the legal basis for non-tax revenue is relatively high in the local government's ordinances, there is considerable autonomy in securing own-source revenues for local finance. As of the 2023 original budget net amount, local non-tax revenue amounts to 24.7 trillion won, accounting for 8.1% of local revenue, which totals 305.4 trillion won. While the total amount of non-tax revenue remains stable from year to year, there are significant variations in specific items by year and region.

2. Categories of Local Non-Tax Revenue

General Accounts and Other Special Accounts

Local non-tax revenue is categorized based on the accounting attribution type into general accounts and special accounts income. It is further divided based on the predictability and stability of revenue into current non-tax revenue, temporary non-tax revenue, and local administrative restriction and levy. Within public enterprise special accounts, revenue is classified differently into business operating revenue and non-business operating revenue based on the content of the revenue. Based on the content of the imposition and collection process, non-tax revenue is divided into imposition and non-imposition non-tax revenue.

In general accounts, current non-tax revenue is collected regularly each year and has a high level of revenue stability. It consists of property rents, service charges, fees, grants to cover tax collection costs, business operating revenue, and interest income, making it the largest source of local non-tax revenue.

Temporary non-tax revenue refers to income that occurs only once in a specific fiscal year, such as property sales revenue, allotment, subsidy return income, and other revenue, as well as previous year's revenue.

Local administrative restriction and levy, on the other hand, represent monetary income imposed and collected as sanctions for violations of laws and non-economic external actions. This category includes penalty, enforcement fine, and allotment.

Local Non-Tax Revenue in Local Public Enterprise Special Accounts

The revenue in local public enterprise special accounts is classified into business operating revenue and non-business operating revenue.

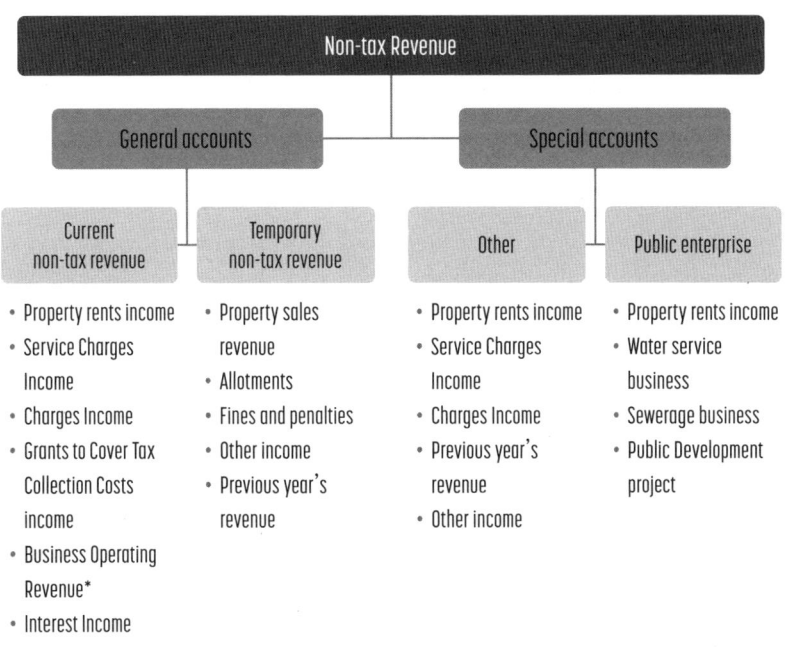

[Figure 2-3] Structure and Types of Local Non-Tax Revenue

※ Business Operating Revenue: parking fee, toll income, liquidation money income, contributions income

Business operating revenue is income obtained by local governments while operating various businesses. It includes income generated from business premises, parking fees, revenue from health centers or medical institutions, various toll fees, replotting liquidation money, contributions from various development projects, and income from the sale of housing, land, and industrial sites. It also includes revenue like water supply revenue for water service, service charge for sewerage business, land sales revenue for public development projects, and loan interest income for the regional development fund.

Non-business operating revenue is a concept similar to temporary non-tax revenue in general accounts(other special accounts). It includes revenue from the sale of capital assets, investment asset revenue, and previous year's revenue, among others.

3. Current Status of Local Non-Tax Revenue

The proportion and trend of local non-tax revenue have varied from year to year. In the mid-1990s, local non-tax revenue accounted for approximately half of local revenue, but by the mid-2020s, it had decreased to around 30%. This shift occurred because local tax and local share tax relatively increased after the revival of local autonomy in 1995, and the proportion of national subsidy rapidly increased after the mid-2000s.

In 2014, the size of non-tax revenue shrank to about one-third compared to the previous year, and its share in local revenue also dropped to the 10% range. This was a numerical phenomenon resulting from the reorganization of the revenue budget subject. The Ministry of Interior and Safety restructured the local revenue items in 2014, separating revenue from carry-over and others(surplus, carry-over, repayment of principal of loan), and internal trading(transferred budget, collection of trust fund, inter-account loan) from the non-tax revenue category and creating separate local revenue items for them.

Within non-tax revenue, the proportions of current non-tax revenue and special account non-tax revenue are relatively high, accounting for 67.6% and 59.1%, respectively, based on the 2023 original budget. Among the revenue items, service charge income and business operating revenue have the highest proportions, representing 41.1% and 11.7% of total non-tax revenue, respectively. Special accounts particularly contribute significantly to these categories. The income proportions of the remaining items are less than 10%.

<Table 2-4> Types of Local Non-Tax Revenue Budget Sizes(2023)

(Unit: billion won, %)

		Size(Net Amount)			Proportion		
		Total	General Accounts	Special Accounts	Total	General Accounts	Special Accounts
Current Non-tax Revenue	Subtotal	166,050	56,914	109,136	67.2	23.0	44.2
	Property Rents Income	9,337	4,455	4,882	3.8	1.8	2.0
	Service Charge Revenue	106,348	16,936	89,412	43.0	6.9	36.2
	Charge Income	20,663	19,692	971	8.4	8.0	0.4
	Business Operating Revenue	19,199	6,958	12,241	7.8	2.8	5.0
	Grants to Cover Tax Collection Costs income	1,274	1,104	170	0.5	0.4	0.1
	Interest Income	9,230	7,769	1,461	3.7	3.1	0.6
Temporary Non-tax Revenue	Subtotal	45,209	37,600	71609	18.3	15.2	29.0
	Property Sales Revenue	8,119	6,883	1,236	3.3	2.8	0.5
	Inter-Municipal Allotment	-	-	-	-	-	-
	Subsidy Return Income	1,626	1,555	71	0.7	0.6	0.0
	Other Revenue	26,759	24,761	1,999	10.8	10.0	0.8
	Previous Year's Revenue	8,704	4,401	4,303	3.5	1.8	1.7
Local Administrative Sanctions · Levy	Subtotal	35,854	8,177	27,678	14.5	3.3	11.2
	Penalty	341	296	45	0.1	0.1	0.0
	Enforcement Fine	1,256	1,156	101	0.5	0.5	0.0
	Compensation Payment	492	324	168	0.2	0.1	0.0
	Penalty	5,207	1,958	3,250	2.1	0.8	0.1
	Redemption Payment	21	19	2	0.0	0.0	1.3
	Allotment	28,515	4,404	24,111	11.5	1.8	0.0
	Statutory Fine	22	20		0.0	0.0	9.8
Total		247,113	102,690	144,423	100	41.6	58.4

Note: Based on the 2023 Original Budget Net Amount
Source: Ministry of Interior and Safety(2023). 2023 Local Government Integrated Financial Overview (Part 1), p.69.

Chapter 2 — · — **Local Revenue and Own-Source**

Chapter 3

Local Revenue and Dependent Financial Resources

Section 1 Local Share Tax

1. The Purpose of the Local Share Tax

The local share tax refers to revenue transferred from the central government to local governments. It operates under the Local Share Tax Act. Local governments enjoy operational flexibility with this revenue because they are not mandated to furnish post-settlement reports to the central government regarding its expenditure. This unique feature grants local governments greater autonomy to allocate local share tax funds. Notably, this taxation mechanism is particularly favored by local governing bodies with lower fiscal capacities because it helps offset financial disparities. Consequently, when redefining the intergovernmental fiscal landscape, the local share tax is the preferred avenue for fiscal adjustment.

The three primary objectives of the local share tax are as follows:

1. To ensure financial security for the basic administrative expenses of local governments.

2. To alleviate the imbalance in own-source income among local governments(disparity adjustment).
3. To maintain, drawing on the purpose of policy management, the linkage between the central government's fiscal expenditure and fiscal management on the one hand and local governments on the other.

The funding allocation formula for the local share tax incorporates the expenditure demands of local finance about nationally driven policies by the central government. Where inappropriate fiscal expenditure issues arise across local finance, it imposes penalties involving reductions in the allocation of local share tax funds.

2. Composition and Funding of the Local Share Tax

General and Special Share Tax

The types of local share tax are classified as general share tax, special share tax, real estate share tax, and fire and security share tax, based on funding sources, allocation methods, and expenditure purposes.

In 2023, funding from the Local Extinction Response Fund was added as a component of the local share tax category for a period of ten years. However, the local share tax has not established any Act that aligns with these regulations. Due to the emerging societal demand for the expansion of local finance, a priority was placed on the values of fiscal equity, which has led to the promotion of financial decentralization through the local share tax system rather than relying solely on local taxes. As a result, starting from the 2000s, new types of local share tax, previously limited to the general and special share tax, have been continuously introduced.

In annually collected national taxes, funding for general and special share taxes takes up 19.24% of the internal tax—97% of these funds constituting the general share tax and 3% the special share tax. The general share tax holds the larger proportion within the local share tax

<Table 3-1> Trends in Revenue Allocation by Local Share Tax Components

(Unit: One hundred million won)

	General Share Tax	Special Share Tax	Real Estate Share Tax	Fire & Security Share Tax	Local Extinction Response Fund	Decentralization Share Tax	Increased Grant	Total
1995	49,857	4,986						54,842
2000	74,687	7,469					510	82,665
2005	179,276	7,116	3,930			8,454		198,775
2010	246,791	9,929	10,221			13,187		280,128
2015	321,762	9,874	14,104	3,141				348,881
2020	449,265	13,895	33,210	6,851				503,221
2021	513,318	15,876	52,153	0,352				591,699
2022	704,142	21,778	75,677	8,853				810,450
2023	666,446	20,612	57,133	8,692	10,000			762,883
Resources	19.24% in internal tax		All of gross real estate tax	45% of individual consumption tax for tobacco	One billion won per year (for 10 years)	Repealed in 2015 (general share tax incorporation)	Repealed in 2015	

Note: Final grant for years before 2022, original budget for 2023.
Source: Ministry of Interior and Safety(2023), 2023 Local Government Integrated Finance Overview(I).

components; the fiscal role of the local share tax is intertwined with the general share tax, serving as the funding source to bridge the financial shortfall—i.e., the difference between standard financial demand and revenue.

The general share tax funds are not allocated to local governments that do not experience a financial shortfall, such as Seoul Metropolitan City. These are referred to as the non-general share tax of local governments. There is an entry for the general share tax category in the revenue budget details of the non-general share tax of local governments. This represents a special funding mechanism whereby an amount equivalent to the disbursed decentralization share tax, following its discontinuation in 2015, is provided to the non-general share tax of local governments as part of the general share tax.

The special share tax serves as an institutional complement to address the failure of the general share tax calculations to capture all the financial demands of local governments. Both the general share tax and the non-general share tax of local governments are eligible to receive the special share tax. The primary factors considered in allocating the special share tax represent disaster and safety management, local issues, and emerging projects requiring collaboration between the central and local governments.

Real Estate Share Tax

The real estate share tax was introduced in 2005, along with the gross real estate tax. Its funding source comes entirely from the gross real estate tax, and it encompasses two societal values: income distribution among different strata and balanced regional development. The process starts by constructing a fair taxation system in the real estate sector and extends to allocating funds for regional balance. This funding nature encompasses both decentralization and balanced development among regions simultaneously.

The criteria for distributing the real estate share tax encompass four standards: fiscal conditions, social welfare demand, regional educational demand, and property tax imposition levels. Basically, the real estate share tax is allocated to local governments. However, even legally categorized metropolitan areas, such as Sejong Self-Governing City and Jeju Self-Governing Province, are included as recipients of the tax distribution. In addition, autonomous districts also receive the real estate share tax due to linkages with property tax. Property tax is a revenue source for autonomous districts when implementing the gross real estate tax.

Fire & Security Share Tax

The fire and security share tax is not provided to local governments but to regional governments. It was introduced as a specific category under the local share tax in 2014, along with the tax increase on tobacco-related products. Its purpose is to secure funds for expanding fire and security facilities and improving emergency management by local governments. The Ministry of Interior and Safety Disaster and Safety Management Headquarters manage these funds. As the central government specifies the purposes of expenditures and the distribution method of these funds, the funds are not technically considered part of the general resources of the local share tax. However, the distinction lies in the fact that the tax does not require settlement reports for the funds allocated to local governments, setting it apart from national subsidies.

Local Extinction Reaction Fund

As concerns about the risk of local extinction persist due to population decline in local governments, an effort is being made to implement local extinction response projects. Responding to this risk, local governments receive 1 trillion Korean won annually for a period of ten years: 25% for metropolitan areas and 75% for local governments. These funds are accounted for under the local share tax category within local revenue.

Funds are provided to 15 regional governments, 89 depopulation areas, and 18 areas of interests, excluding Seoul Metropolitan City and Sejong Self-Governing City. For regional governments, allocation considers factors such as the population decline index, fiscal conditions, and demographic conditions; for local governments, specific allocation strategies are determined after assessing investment plans.

3. General Share Tax and Adjustments

The Distribution Formula

The Ministry of Interior and Safety annually calculates the standard amount of financial demand and the standard amount of financial revenue for each local government, ensuring the preservation of the "financial shortfall," which represents demand exceeding income. The standard amount of financial demand refers to the "general" amount of financial demand for each local government, calculated on a reasonable criterion. Correspondingly, the standard amount of financial revenue reflects the "general" amount of financial revenue for each local government, determined by a reasonable criterion to evaluate a local government's fiscal capacity.

The total funding amount of the general share tax is fixed at a certain proportion of internal tax. If there is a disparity between the local government's financial shortfalls and the available fund size, then an adjustment rate is uniformly applied to determine the distributed amount of the general share tax for each local government. In this respect, the general share tax does not guarantee preserving the entire financial shortfalls for local governments. Since the revenue from internal tax varies annually, the adjustment rate is inconsistent year to year.

The Special Provision of 3% for Jeju Self-Governing Province

The calculation method for Jeju Self-Governing Province's general share tax funding is distinct from the others. Before its transition into a Special Self-Governing Province, Jeju Island consisted of four local governments — Jeju City, Seogwipo City, Southern Jeju County Office, and Northern Jeju County — under the regional government of Jeju

Province. Each local government received its respective allocation of the general share tax. However, these local governments were incorporated into a single regional government after their conversion into a Special Self-Governing Province. Consequently, 3% of the total general share tax funding is initially provided at a flat rate, preventing disadvantages in the general share tax distribution due to the consolidation of Jeju's local governments.

[Figure 3-1] Distribution Formula for the General Share Tax

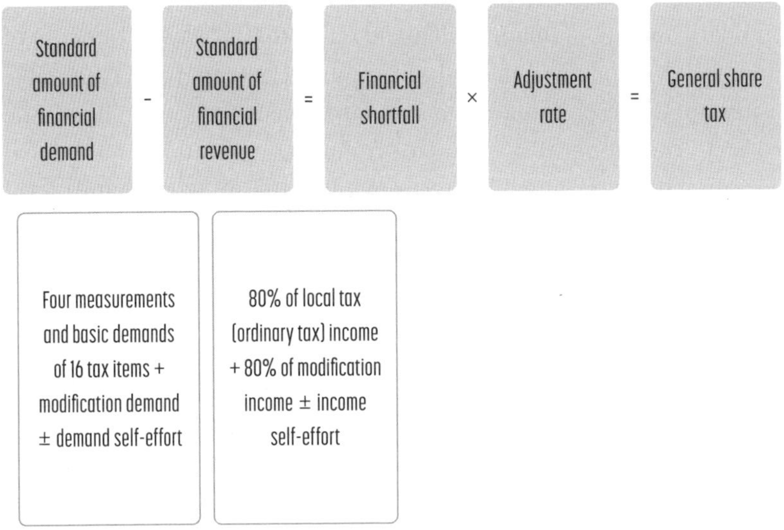

Standard amount of financial demand	−	Standard amount of financial revenue	=	Financial shortfall	×	Adjustment rate	=	General share tax
Four measurements and basic demands of 16 tax items + modification demand ± demand self-effort		80% of local tax (ordinary tax) income + 80% of modification income ± income self-effort						

4. Policy Goals of Local Share Tax System

Relationship between Adjustment and Local Share Tax

Local tax and local share tax, as pivotal revenue sources, arise in any discussion of the various policy discourses such as decentralization, financial security, and addressing financial gaps between local

<Table 3-2> Trend of Distribution in General Share Tax

(Unit: Hundred thousand, %)

	Including Non-General Share Tax Local Government			Exempting Non-General Share Tax Local Government					
	Standard Amount of Financial Demand	Standard Amount of Financial Revenue	Fiscal Capacity Index	Standard Amount of Financial Demand	Standard Amount of Financial Revenue	Financial Shortfall	General 1) Share Tax	Jeju 2) (3%)	Adjustment Rate (3%)
2015	835,202	485,317	0.58	705,488	349,684	355,804	321,762	9,653	86.3
2017	956,852	592,044	0.62	757,850	373,166	384,685	387,397	11,622	94.0
2019	1,262,443	769,743	0.61	1,000,399	470,114	530,285	476,026	14,282	86.4
2021	1,360,141	795,818	0.59	1,104,377	533,572	570,805	445,377	13,361	75.1
2022	1,541,288	1,002,670	0.65	1,214,619	597,694	616,925	551,042	16,531	86.0
2023	1,818,609	1,155,814	0.64	1,478,110	690,393	787,717	666,446	19,993	81.6

Note: 1) Total amount of allocated general share tax; 2) Preferential allocation of 3% of general share tax;
3) adjustment rate = (general share tax − Jeju's 3%) × 100 / financial shortfall
Source: Ministry of Interior and Safety [Calculation Details of general share tax.]

governments. For example, when the government pursues financial decentralization through local tax, it must concurrently manage fiscal equity in underprivileged regions.

However, there's a risk, especially in financially disadvantaged regions, of a moral hazard arising from excessive reliance on local share tax from the central government without making an effort to secure the extent of self-generated revenue. Another concern arises from the phenomenon of excessive equity based on the disparity between the order of fiscal independence and fiscal autonomy after the distribution of local share tax.

Adjustment and Fiscal Management Functions

In discussions about enhancing the inherent functions of the local share tax system and improving the newly introduced fiscal functions, the primary concern is the level of financial security. The types and scale of basic expenditure that the central government is supposed to ensure have continued to expand, while the total amount is legalized by a fixed proportion of internal tax. Therefore, the fiscal adjustment rate has become inconsistent year by year, weakening the function of financial security.

In addition, the policy function of the central government has been criticized for having an excessive influence on the modification demand considered when calculating the standard amount of financial demand for the general share tax. As a result, one primary concern is that the nature of the general share tax funding becomes heavily influenced by the characteristics of a national subsidy, weakening its original role of providing general resources to local governments.

The final concern is about the adequacy of the Ministry of Interior and Safety's implementation of the local share tax reduction review system. How this system operates—and the corresponding rules and regulations—raises concerns about the possibility of unduly diminishing the self-governance of local finance.

Section 2 Adjustment Grant and Regional Coexistent Development Fund

1. City & County Adjustment Grant

The City & County Adjustment Grant is a general resource that allocates a portion of the provincial tax revenue to city & county. It not only serves as a vertical fiscal adjustment between metropolitan and local levels but also horizontally addresses fiscal disparities between city & county. The current system largely aligns with the former aspect. However, recent provincial government offices have been strengthening their role in adjusting fiscal disparities between city & county. Provincial government manage the adjustment grant system, drawing upon Article 29 of the Local Finance Act and the Adjustment Grants Allocation Ordinance in each city and province. Busan, Daegu, and Incheon, where "County" is established within local governments, operate the city & county adjustment grant system.

The purpose of City & County Adjustment Grants differs from that of the autonomous district adjustment grant. The primary objective is not only to achieve fiscal equity between Metropolitan(Provincial Government) and local(city & county) levels but also to fill the gap of fiscal disparities across city & county. Unlike autonomous districts, city & county collect local taxes across multiple categories while receiving the general share tax from the central government. Therefore, in terms of institutional structure, the Provincial Government does not need to perform the function of financial security to meet the basic demands of city & county. Indeed, the primary function of the autonomous district adjustment grant is to ensure the standard amount of financial demand.

2. Autonomous District Adjustment Grants

The autonomous districts in Seoul and other local metropolitan cities

<Table 3-3> Resource Allocation Method Change in City & County Adjustment Grant

	Name	Type	General Fiscal Compensation Fund Distribution	Source	Add
1999	Grants to Cover Tax Collection Costs		Province Tax of City & County Collection Performance	· General City & County, Province Tax, 30% · Population over 50 million, 50%	
2000			· Population 60% · Collection Performance 40%	· Province Tax of City & County 27% · Population over 50 million, 47% · 3% Grants to Cover Tax Collection Costs · Excluded Province Tax · Common Facilities tax	· Distribution of Gyeonggi-Province General Fiscal Compensation Fund 25% as Special Fiscal Compensation Fund
2006	Fiscal Compensation Fund	· General Fiscal Compensation Fund 90% · Measure Compensation Fund 10%		· (Basic resource same) · Excluded Province Tax · Common Facilities Tax · Local Education Tax	· 70% of Cyeonggi-Province Special Fiscal Compensation Fund · Prioritizing Distribution to the Population under 20 million(2013 abolition)
2007			· Population 50% · Collection Performance 40% · Fiscal Capacity Index 10%	· (Basic resource same) · Excluded Province Tax. · Common Facilities Tax · Local Education Tax · Regional Development Tax for Nuclear Power Generation	· Distribution of 65% of Regional Development Tax for Nuclear Power Generation to each City & County
2010				Local Consumption Tax 27% add	Local Consumption Tax is Distributed by the Population of City & County
2014	Adjustment Grant	· General Adjustment Grant 90% special Adjustment Grant 10%	· Population 50% · Collection Performance 30% · Fiscal Capacity Index 20%	· (Basic resource same) · Excluded Province Tax · Local Education Tax · Taxation on Real Estate	· Not Using Special Sharing Fund as Subsidy Projects Resource · General Share Tax · Non-general Share Tax · Local Government Preferential Allocation Special Cases
2016			· Population 50% · Collection Performance 20% · Fiscal Capacity Index 30%	· Local Resource and Facility Tax · Thermal Power, Nuclear Power Generation Local Resource and Facility Tax	· General Share Tax · Non-general Share Tax · Local Government Preferential Allocation · Special Cases Abolition

receive adjustment grants as unrestricted general resources from the main office of their respective city. Through an amendment of the Local Autonomy Act in 1988, each metropolitan city established autonomous districts. The introduction of the adjustment grant system aimed to provide financial support to autonomous districts in the form of general resources from the city's main office and to facilitate fund adjustment among autonomous districts within the jurisdiction.

The operational principles of the system are similar to those of the general share tax system. The principal assumptions were to ensure financial security for autonomous districts' financial demand and to mitigate fiscal capacity disparities among autonomous districts. Adjustment grants are divided into general adjustment grants and special adjustment grants, with the latter accounting for 10% of the total adjustment grants. The funding source for adjustment grants comes from some proportions of "ordinary tax" by city main offices, but each local government has different disbursement rates. Gwangju Metropolitan City has the highest at 23.9%, and Incheon and Ulsan show the lowest at 20%.

3. Regional Coexistent Development Fund

The Regional Coexistent Development Fund is based on Article 17 of the Local Government Fund Management Basic Act. Since its enactment in 2006, it has allowed local governments to establish a Regional Development Cooperation Fund using surplus funds from inter-local governments. This initiative aims to manage and utilize surplus funds efficiently and to bring mutual benefits.

The establishment of the Regional Coexistent Development Fund as it exists today followed the Ministry of Interior and Safety's "Restructuring Plan for Local Finance Support System," announced in September 2009. The funds for this initiative were arranged by allocating 35% of the total local consumption tax of regional governments in metropolitan areas, starting in 2010 and continuing for a period of 10 years.

Through an amendment to the Local Government Fund Management Basic Act in 2010, the fund was re-named "Regional Coexistent Development Fund." Its funding sources were expanded to include local bond issuance revenue, local government contributions, and contributions from public corporations, in addition to local consumption tax contributions. However, the majority of contributions come from the local consumption tax contributions of local governments in metropolitan areas even if various forms of fund resources can be used from a legal perspective.

The Regional Coexistent Development Fund was abolished under a sunset clause. However, with the second phase of financial decentralization during the Moon Jae-in Administration, a mandatory contribution to the funds from local governments in metropolitan areas was reinstated. Following an additional local transfer from value-added tax(expanding the local consumption tax), local governments in metropolitan areas now contribute 35% of the net increase in the transfer amount to the Regional Coexistent Development Fund.

The Regional Coexistent Development Fund is distributed and managed into a loan management account and a financial support account. The financial support account refers to financial assistance and support for supplementary projects to local governments, allowing comprehensive expenditures on regional development-related initiatives. While limited to job creation projects in 2010, the scope of expenditures was significantly expanded from 2012.

4. Policy Goals of AG & RCDF

The adjustment grant(AG) and the Regional Coexistent Development Fund(RCDF) share the characteristics of horizontal fiscal adjustment in terms of intergovernmental fund transfer. According to the Local Autonomy Act, metropolitan areas and local governments show an

<Table 3-4> Account of Regional Coexistent Development Fund

	Subject	Resource
Financial Support Account	Regional Development Projects · Regional employment improvement · Local economic development · Encouraging childbirth and infant childcare services · Environmental development (culture, education, health, etc.) · Inter-regional collaboration	· Metropolitan area Si and Province Contribution · Financial support account revenues accruing from the operation · Loan management account transferred money
Loan Management Account	· Long-term low-interest loans · Local governments · Local corporation · Public corporation	· Local governments fund deposit · Local bond issuance revenue and temporary borrowing · Local government contributions · Contributions of public corporations with local governments as members · Revenues accruing from the operation by loan management account

equal legal status, implying that the adjustment grant of City & County can be understood as a mechanism for horizontal fiscal adjustment, where metropolitan and local governments use revenue from local taxes collaboratively. On the other hand, in the context of the Local Finance Act, regional governments are granted authority to manage and oversee the fiscal functions of local governments. Therefore, from a fiscal perspective, the interpretation of horizontal fiscal adjustment takes on a different meaning.

In this respect, there is a challenge to clearly define the legal nature of the adjustment grant system within local finance. While the Local Finance Act has defined the purpose of the adjustment grant as being to address fiscal disparities among local governments, the actual implementation of the system has limited the functions of the disparity adjustment. The City & County adjustment grants have shown the nature of the shared tax between the Provincial Government Office and City & County. An autonomous district adjustment grant places a greater emphasis on providing financial security for the administrative expenses of autonomous districts.

City & County adjustment grants are supposed to clarify the characteristics of fiscal adjustment between the province and City & County and to set up an appropriate balance. In the case of autonomous district adjustment grants, they should expand the financial security function to address funding shortfalls. Aligned with this, they need to carry out simultaneous adjustments to the fiscal functions between the city's main office and autonomous districts, as well as between the city subsidy and the adjustment grant.

The Regional Coexistent Development Fund is a horizontal fiscal adjustment fund with the characteristics of interregional collaboration, where local governments in metropolitan areas share a portion of their local consumption tax revenue with all local governments. In enhancing this feature, it is necessary to strengthen the regional collaborative nature within fund projects. Instead of limiting the fund contributions to local governments within the metropolitan areas, all nationwide local governments need to contribute funds. This contribution can facilitate the function of interregional collaborative resources, encouraging joint investments across regions and sharing social service facilities.

Section 3 Subsidy

1. The Purpose of Subsidy

Subsidy and Local Finance

The subsidy serves as both a "local" source of funding to ensure local government revenue and a "central" source of funding that imposes accountability on local government expenditure. While referred to as a "national subsidy" in terms of local revenue, it is denoted as a "national subsidy project" in the context of expenditure. Consequently, the financial characteristics of revenue and expenditure can be configured differently. Subsidy is a complex concept that considers not only the entire amount of financial funding but also various characteristics in functional and individual project approaches.

The proportion of national subsidies in the revenue of local finance continues to increase. For example, when arranging their budgets and considering new investment projects, local governments prioritize whether they can receive national subsidies from the central government. Failing to secure national or state funding makes it difficult for local governments to plan and undertake their own independent projects.

The Fiscal Characteristics of the National Subsidy Source

The fiscal characteristics of the national subsidy source contain several negative factors. In a decentralized national system, national subsidy projects may carry moral hazards due to the demarcation line between decision-making and implementation, resulting in a principal–agent problem. The central government faces information asymmetry when there is insufficient information regarding financial demands for subsidy projects and their implementation. As a result, it cannot be guaranteed that the original policy intentions will be properly implemented.

Based on the perspective of local governments, the national subsidy by the central government functions as a form of common resource. This may allow predatory competition focused solely on attracting funding for subsidies, potentially leading to the tragedy of the commons in fiscal management. When the central government designs fiscal initiatives that consider not only its own but also local resources, the national subsidy may threaten government fiscal expansion through the flypaper effect. As the central government strengthens vertical control mechanisms for the efficient management of national subsidies and individual grant programs, fiscal inefficiency could worsen. The central government aims to encourage local governments to implement projects proactively to enhance project outcomes and achieve maximum impact. However, local governments often adopt a passive approach, only meeting the central government's minimum standards.

2. National Subsidy Trends

The national subsidy constitutes the largest share of local revenue, amounting to 160.1 trillion KRW based on the original budget gross amount in local finance. Over the past two decades, the local revenue structure has become entrenched in a central dependent type. In 2000, subsidies accounted for 21.5% of the total, but this figure had risen to 37.8 by 2023, creating a significant gap between the gross and net amounts of subsidies.

Based on the net amount, subsidies were 77.8 trillion KRW, indicating a gap of 82.3 trillion KRW compared with the gross amount. The part of Double Count A is greater than the net amount due to instances where the same subsidy is calculated redundantly between regional government and local government or among various local governments. A high level of redundancy implies inefficiencies within fiscal management.

The distribution of national subsidies transferred from various ministries and agencies of the central government to local governments concentrates in certain departments. Notably, the top eight departments, such as the Ministry of Health and Welfare and the Ministry of Land, Infrastructure and Transport, account for 93.4% of the total funding resource.

<Table 3-5> Trends in the Composition of Local Government Revenue

(Unit: %, 100 million KRW)

	2000(A)	2005	2010	2015	2020	2023(B)	(B)-(A)
Local tax	26.2	28.6	26.1	25.8	26.8	27.6	1.4
Non-tax revenue	29.8	24.8	21.5	9.2	7.6	6.4	
Local share tax	10.0	14.6	13.9	13.5	14.3	15.0	4.9
Adjustment grant etc.	3.1	4.3	3.3	3.2	3.2	3.2	0.1
Subsidy	21.5	24.5	31.6	35.6	36.0	37.8	16.2
Local bond	4.5	3.2	3.5	2.2	1.6	0.7	-3.8
Revenue from Carry-over and others	4.8	-	-	10.6	10.5	9.3	
Total	100.0	100.0	100.0	100.0	100.0	100.0	
(Amount)	706,934	1,177,417	1,832,261	2,339,516	3,450,197	4,239,409	

Note: General & Special Account Gross Amount
Source: Local finance 365(http://lofin.mois.go.kr)

3. The Rates of Subsidies in National Subsidy Projects

Standard Rate of Subsidies

The fiscal relationship and allocation of fiscal responsibilities between the central and local governments in national subsidy projects are established through the standard rates of subsidies system. The rates for all departments of the central government are compiled in Appendix 1 of the Enforcement Decree of the Subsidy Management Act. Not all national subsidy projects have their standard rates of subsidies legalized. For projects beyond those covered by the legally defined standard rates, each central department has a discretion for national subsidy projects to determine their respective rates. Most cases are determined to the extent analogous to the legalized standard rate for each field or project.

Among the national subsidy projects, those specifying the standard rates of subsidies in an enforcement decree constitute only about 10% of all national subsidy projects. In addition, a lack of consistency is shown in the level of subsidy rates on fiscal functions. The prevalence of an excessively low standard rate, falling below 50%, exacerbates the phenomenon of imposing local resources on top-down projects. Either the project-related Act managed by each government department or the budget-related Act managed by the fiscal authorities can define the standard rates of subsidies legalized. Japan adopts the former approach, whereas the system in South Korea falls under the latter(except for the basic pension). Whether to explicitly stipulate standard rates of subsidies in the legislative process or leave them to the discretion of each department is also a contentious issue.

Dual Rate of Welfare Subsidies between Seoul and Others

Social welfare projects show the distinct characteristics of financial resource allocation, applying a relatively lower standard rate of subsidies to Seoul Metropolitan City compared with local governments. As of 2017, among 121 social welfare projects, only 47 applied the same subsidy rate as local governments, while the remaining 74 projects employed a decreased subsidy rate. In addition, the level of differentiation varied across projects. One project presented 15%, 33.3%, and 40% disparities; some projects showed a 20% or 30% gap.

These differentiations are also evident in each social welfare sector. In childcare services, where standard rates of subsidies are inherently low, 17 of 28 projects were subject to a differentiated standard rate of subsidy. Among these, nine exhibited a 30% gap in subsidy rates. On the other hand, 14 projects out of 22 in elder-care services employed the same subsidy rate, providing a marked contrast to the childcare sector.

The differentiation of the standard rate of subsidies in Seoul Metropolitan City may hinder smooth collaboration between the Ministry of Health and Welfare and Seoul Metropolitan City when delivering regional welfare services.

Differential Subsidy Ratio Utilizing Index Calculation

Projects of basic livelihood security benefits(except for medical benefits), childcare services, and the basic pension apply to the differential subsidy ratio through index calculation. The subsidy ratio in the basic pension is defined in the Enforcement Decree of the Basic Pension Act and falls under the jurisdiction of the Ministry of Health and Welfare. In contrast, the differential subsidy ratio for other social welfare projects, such as basic livelihood security, is stipulated in the table of the Enforcement Decree of the Subsidy Management Act under the jurisdiction of the Ministry of Economy and Finance.

There are significant differences in the operational characteristics of the differential subsidy ratio between basic pension projects managed by the Ministry of Health and Welfare and the basic livelihood security benefit falling under the Ministry of Economy and Finance. The Ministry of Economy and Finance establishes a standard subsidy rate for each project and applies a 10% decrease or increase subsidy ratio. A decreased subsidy ratio is limited to general share tax, non-general share tax, and local government. In this respect, the increased subsidy ratio is subject to significant debate concerning the scope and scale of local governments where it is applicable.

In the case of the basic pension project overseen by the Ministry of Health and Welfare, the standard subsidy rate varies from 40% to 90% based on fiscal autonomy and the aging rate. Using the objective indicator of the aging rate allows for equity in applying the differential subsidy ratio across different types of local governments. On the other hand, the differential subsidy ratio for basic livelihood security utilizes the social service expenditure index, so it does not guarantee equity. In particular, while City & County are subject to relatively disadvantageous

<Table 3-6> Criteria for Applying Differential Subsidy Ratio

			<Basic livelihood security, Childcare>			<Basic pension>			<Expansion of Youth facilities>
			Social Services Expenditures Index			Elder Population Ratio			
			20% below	20% or more 25% below	25% or more	14% below	14% or more 20% below	20% above	
Fiscal Autonomy	90% or more					40	50	60	Seoul Metropolitan City : 30 local: 70-88 (Differentiation based on fiscal autonomy)
	80% or more 90% below	85% or more	10% decrease	Standard rate of subsidies	Standard rate of subsidies	50	60	70	
		85% below 80% or more	Standard rate of subsidies	Standard rate of subsidies	Standard rate of subsidies				
	80% below		Standard rate of subsidies	Standard rate of subsidies	10% increase	70	80	90	

Source: Enforcement Decree of the Subsidy Management Act table 3, Enforcement Decree of Basic Pension Act table 2.

provisions, autonomous districts have a structural advantage because they have not only low fiscal autonomy but also high social service expenditures.

4. Balanced Regional Development Special Account

The Ministry of Economy and Finance has been operating the Balanced Regional Development Special Account since 2005, which supports the specialized development of regions with their comparative advantages and encourages projects aimed at improving the quality of life for local residents and regional competitiveness. The official name has undergone changes over different administrations.

The Local Autonomous Account in the Balanced Regional Development Special Account has allowed local governments to select specific individual projects and to allocate funds to each project autonomously, after funds have been allocated to local governments in a lump sum. As a result, it shows the characteristic of a "block grant," which distinguishes it from the funding allocation approach of typical national subsidy projects.

Particularly in the Local Autonomous Account local governments autonomously allocate funds for specific projects within the allocated total fund range. However, the management and supervision of each project are entrusted to each central government department. In addition, the National Assembly's budget review of the Balanced Regional Development Special Account falls under the Strategy and Finance Committee, while each project related to expenditures is handled by the relevant standing committee.

Each central department and the National Assembly standing committee only review the details of commissioned projects; it does not have the authority to allocate funds. The projects within the Balanced Regional Development Special Account are separately managed as

<Table 3-7> Structure of Balanced Regional Development Special Account

Account Compilation			Local Autonomous Account	Local Support Account	Sejong Special Self-Governing City Account	Jeju Special Self-Governing Province Account
Local Government Autonomous Budgeting	Regional Government		① Regional Government Autonomous Budgeting Projects	-	③ Regional Government Local Government Autonomous Budgeting Projects * Local Government Infrastructure Development Projects, etc.	④ Regional Government, City & County Guautonomous Budgeting Projects * Local Government Infrastructure Development Projects, etc. ⑤ Special Local Administrationagency Delegated Affairs Operating Expense
	Local Government		② Local Government Autonomous Budgeting Projects	-		
Department Budgeting			-	⑥ Department Budgeting Projects	⑦ Department Budgeting Projects	⑧ Department Budgeting Projects

distinct items in the budgetary document of each central department. Therefore, their accounting structure may hinder comprehensive management of project outcomes within the overall framework of the budgetary process.

5. Policy Agenda in the Subsidy System

Establishing a New Platform in Inter-governmental Fiscal Relations

A fundamental shift in the assumptions underlying national subsidies and national subsidy projects is necessary to establish a new platform for an intergovernmental fiscal relationship. Three key premises are crucial.

First, it is essential to establish that national subsidies are not merely benevolent transfers from the central government but are local revenues. Second, intergovernmental fiscal relations necessitate a problem-solving approach through outcome-oriented accountability. Third, the establishment of a horizontal collaborative partnership among governments must ensure local autonomy.

The national subsidy system faces several criticisms through the lens of fiscal management. For instance, there could be a digital divide, moral hazards, flypaper effects and fiscal expansion, a hierarchical structure and cartel in fiscal projects, the deadweight loss by a territorial monopoly, and vulnerability in outcome-oriented performance management. The key policy challenge in response is to reduce the number and scale of national subsidies and national subsidy projects. In this regard, critical national subsidy projects need to become state affairs if they should be operated at all, regardless of local financial conditions. On the other hand, various projects managed by local governments should be local government's inherent affairs, transferring them to local government as an innovation of financial decentralization.

Strengthening the Central Government's Fiscal Functioning

The fiscal role of the central government must be bolstered. This will improve the stability of citizens' livelihoods and develop social infrastructure. The four basic welfare programs refer to livelihood benefits, medical benefits, the basic pension, and childcare services. Transitioning the final delivery of a basic livelihood security service from local governments to the central government as state affairs can lead to increased administrative efficiency. In particular, integrating livelihood benefits, the basic pension, and medical benefits into the national pension and health insurance systems holds the potential for a new societal policy that guarantees the income and health of the entire population, irrespective of economic vulnerability, through a combination of social insurance and budgetary resources.

Revitalizing the Problem-Solving Approach in Subsidy Rate

Within the hierarchical management framework of central, metropolitan, and local levels, the detailed specification of standard rates of subsidies on a project-by-project basis may fail to serve as an effective means of addressing societal problems.

Shifting the perspective of institutional reform from the current "fiscal management"-oriented approach to a "problem solving"-oriented approach could offer new alternatives.

If the current intergovernmental fiscal relationship system is maintained, the standard rates of subsidies would need to be reconfigured based on the specific characteristics of each subsidy project.

Considering the nature of policies inherent in the project's characteristics and decentralized attributes of local government discretion, the standard rates of subsidies for projects that require nationwide adherence to the central government's guidelines should be increased beyond current levels. On the other hand, for projects with substantial local government discretion and those supported by the central government for incentivizing purposes, lower subsidy rates should be established. These projects should undergo regular sunset-clause assessments and be gradually transferred to local control.

The validity of the existing rules for differential subsidy ratios should be reevaluated, and a new approach should consider a method for integrating the standard rate of subsidy system into a new one. In social welfare projects where a 10% increased subsidy ratio is applied in most autonomous districts, it is necessary to incorporate the practical outcomes of the differential subsidy ratio into the standard rate of subsidies to enhance the efficiency of the institutional operation.

Establishing horizontal cross-subsidy mechanisms among local governments, such as the Regional Coexistent Development Fund, can fill the gap of fiscal disparities. In addition, national subsidy projects need to design an alternative that applies consistent standard rates of subsidies based on the nature of the projects.

Strengthening Accountability for BND-SA

National subsidy projects within the Local Autonomous Account of the Balanced National Development Special Account(BND-SA) require a comprehensive reassessment. Despite emphasizing the balance in its name, the actual allocation of funds demonstrates an imbalance, with a greater distribution to the metropolitan areas. This is because the Ministry of Economy and Finance is directly involved in each project, deviating from the fundamental principles of fiscal management. While management of the overall fiscal amount of the Balanced National Development Special Account may be feasible, the accountability for performance in each project remains weak.

Establishing a Tailored Management of Subsidy Projects

There is a need for a shift in the national subsidy and national subsidy management system through the fiscal characteristics of national subsidy projects. The existing subsidy management systems established in the mid-1980s are not well-suited to the current era. With over a thousand national subsidy projects exhibiting varying fiscal characteristics, including National Allotment, National Contributions, National Subsidy, and National Deposit, a diverse range of types exists. Considering the different fiscal relationship characteristics between the central and local levels for each type, it is necessary to establish tailored management systems for each subsidy project or subsidy fund management.

Chapter 4

Local Bond

Section 1 Definition and Types of Local Bonds

1. Definition of Local Bonds

Local bonds are debts incurred by local governments for a specific period and secured by their taxation rights to address a funding shortfall. They are borrowed from the public or private sectors and spread over multiple fiscal years. Local governments facing financial demands they can't meet through their own source and transfer revenue issue local bonds to mobilize investment resources.

Within local revenue, issuing local bonds is restrained as an exceptional funding source. Local governments issue local bonds under specific limits for each local government, such as emergency disaster recovery or enduring benefit, or under approval from the Ministry of Interior and Safety and local council.

Local bonds serve as a source of revenue for local finance. In addition, local bonds have an intergenerational resource-sharing effect. For instance, in cases where the benefits of investments such as roads or water supply facilities extend beyond the current generation to future generations, using local bonds alongside local taxes enhances the responsiveness of benefits and cost-sharing between generations, creating an equitable intergenerational resource-sharing effect. Last, local bonds serve the function of preserving deficit finances. Local governments can enhance the flexibility of fiscal management and increase discretion, providing a path to using local bonds when funds are insufficient to meet financial demands.

2. Types of Local Bonds based on the Purposes

Local bonds are categorized into General Accounts Bonds, Public Enterprise Special Account Bonds, and Other Special Account Bonds based on the purpose of borrowing.

First, General Accounts Bonds serve as funds for general accounts and aim to support social welfare projects, road and bridge construction, water supply infrastructure, transportation, housing and land development, agricultural land development, commercial facilities, facilities management, tourism complex development, and cultural facilities.

Second, Public Enterprise Special Account Bonds are debts raised from the funds of local public enterprises. They are issued for projects conducted under local public enterprise special accounts, such as water supply and sewage, subway system, housing and land development, and other public development initiatives.

Third, Other Special Account Bonds are sourced from other special account funds and are issued for specific projects similar to public enterprise special account bonds. These projects include housing and land development, agricultural and industrial complex development, new town development, tourism, and leisure complex development.

<Table 4-1> Local Bonds by Local Governments(2021)

(Unit: 100 million KRW)

Region	Total	General Accounts	Other Special Accounts	Public Enterprise Special Accounts	Funds
Seoul	115,342	342	107,500	0	7,500
Busan	32,338	17,505	11,228	0	3,606
Daegu	23,735	7,671	2,993	400	12,672
Incheon	20,516	10,596	2,595	128	7,197
Gwangju	12,548	7,838	0	29	4,681
Daejeon	8,476	4,241	200	0	4,036
Ulsan	9,884	2,806	500	0	6,578
Sejong	3,729	1,427	307	0	1,996
Gyeonggi	30,204	8,325	1,376	0	20,503
Gangwon	13,650	4,165	355	90	9,040
Chungbuk	9,190	1,288	80	50	7,772
Chungnam	11,883	6,148	77	0	5,658
Jeonbuk	8,105	2,533	180	44	5,349
Jeonam	14,754	2,640	100	0	12,014
Gyeongbuk	17,977	5,826	546	89	11,516
Gyeongnam	16,688	10,249	1,857	235	4,347
Jeju	10,462	7,198	35	300	2,929
Total	359,481	100,796	129,929	1,365	127,392

Source: Ministry of Interior and Safety(2022), "2021 local debt status."

3. Types of Local Bonds with Bond Issuance Method

Certificate Borrowing Goods

The term "certificate borrowing goods" refers to the practice whereby local governments enter into agreements with the central government, public institutions, or financial institutions to borrow funds and issue and submit certificates of indebtedness. Local governments often utilize certificate borrowing goods to borrow government or financial funds easily. The central government provides various funds such as the Public Management Fund. Local public funds include the Building Maintenance Fund and the Regional Coexistent Development Fund operated by the local finance association, as well as the Regional Development Fund handled by the province's main office. Private funds refer to certificates of indebtedness obtained through loans from commercial banks and non-bank depository institutions.

Domestically and through public loan commercial credit, funds can come from foreign sources. Until the 1990s, developing countries employed policy funds known as public loans. However, since 1995, South Korea has been excluded from the list of countries eligible for the support of borrowing goods. Commercial credit refers to the funds involved in contracts with foreign entities to borrow resources.

Security Issue Bonds

"Security issue bonds" refers to the issue of bonds with a coupon interest rate similar to a corporate fund. Based on the intended recipients of the issuance, securities issue bonds can be categorized into public loans, sales bonds, and government compensation bonds.

Public loans represent a bond issued to the general public, similar to corporate funds, wherein cash is collected by attracting diverse investors and issuing securities. Second, sales bonds involve the mandatory purchase of some portions of the local bond by residents receiving administrative services, such as permits or vehicle registration from local governments. For instance, it refers to Urban Railway Bonds, water and sewerage bonds, and Regional Development Public Bonds. Third, government compensation bonds are bonds issued to creditors by local governments in order to commit to deferred cash payments for purposes such as land acquisition or meeting construction expenses. In return, local bond securities are allocated to creditors, ensuring repayment at a predetermined future date.

Until the 1990s, when domestic market interest rates were relatively high, there were instances of incorporating foreign bonds that provided good repayment periods and interest rates. However, following the IMF crisis of the late 1990s, the risks associated with exchange rate fluctuations escalated. In the 2000s, domestic interest rates rapidly declined. These changes in the economic environment gradually diminished the reliance on foreign bonds and funds.

Section 2 Local Bond Management System

1. Management of Local Bonds by MOIS

Management of Eligible Projects for Local Bond Issuance

In managing local bonds, the Ministry of Interior and Safety operates a guideline for projects eligible for local bond issuance. According to this guideline, local governments may issue local bonds for capital expenditure projects, but issuing local bonds for consumable current expenditures, such as maintenance costs, general research expenses, and goods expenses, as well as personal expenses, is prohibited.

There are four types of eligible projects for issuing local bonds:

1. Fiscal investment projects such as the establishment of public property and subordinated finances to cover associated expenses
2. Disaster prevention and recovery projects
3. Preservation of revenue deficit by unforeseen natural disasters
4. The conversion of local bonds.

Even for the projects that fall under the categories eligible for local bond issuance, there are limitations on issuing local bonds for projects below a certain scale that are subject to fiscal investment review. Specifically, in terms of total project costs, a project less than 4 billion KRW for metropolitan and province areas and less than 2 billion KRW for the Si, Gun, and Gu areas cannot issue local bonds. However, there is an exception for small-scale local government facility projects financed by the Building Maintenance Fund.

Management of Local Bond Issuance Limits

The central government tends to control local bond issuance due to the prevalent perception that local bonds are not generally recognized as regular budgetary funds but as exceptional funding.

Local governments can engage in actions that result in issuing local bonds or other forms of debt within a certain limit, subject to approval by the local council. However, if the issuance exceeds this limit, prior approval from the Ministry of Interior and Safety is required. In the case of foreign bonds managing the risks of foreign exchange, even if they fall within the limit range, approval from the Ministry of Interior and Safety must be obtained before seeking approval from the local council.

The Ministry of Interior and Safety annually determines the limit for local bond issuance, taking into account the financial situation of each local government, such as the scale of debt and repayment schedule, etc. This limit is set within 10% of the local government's budget for two years prior. The limit of local bond issuance varies based on local government hierarchies, such as metropolitan cities with a population of over one million and Local Government.

There are regulations regarding the priority of fulfilling the issuance limit, adjustment, and eligibility, even within the established limit. For local public enterprises, distinct criteria for local bond issuance are applied, taking into consideration the nature of the eligible projects and other relevant factors.

<Table 4-2> Criteria for Calculating Local Bond Limit Based on Types of Local Governments

Subject		Regional Government, Metropolitan City over One Million Population	Local Government
Total limit (A+B)	Basic Limit (A)	〖Ordinary general revenue-(general debt+BTL rent+contingent liabilities 50%)〗×10%	
	Metropolitan Special Case	Additional 10% with Basic limit	
	Distinct Limit (B)	Regional Development Bond Urban Railway Bonds Issue amount + '2023 conversion issue amount + Local Employment Projects(Investment projects) + long-term unexecuted urban planning facility	

Source: Ministry of Interior and Safety(2022) "2023 local bond issue plan establishment criteria."

2. Local Bond Management by Local Governments

The Local Autonomy Act establishes the fundamental principle of financial management as fiscal health. In fact, Article 122 explicitly states, "Local governments must operate their finanies in a healthy manner in accordance with the principle of a balanced budget." Furthermore, the Local Finance Act provides specific regulations regarding the eligibility of projects, limitations on issuance, and the issuance procedure, thereby overseeing the management of local bond issuance.

In local finances, local bonds take up approximately 1% of the total budget each year. The scope of projects and sources of funds for bond floatation are defined as specific sectors, thus helping prevent excessive local finance operations caused by such local bonds and contributing to responsible financial management.

Section 3 Future Tasks for Local Bond Management

1. Enhancing the Utilization Strategies of Local Bonds

Local governments have been relatively passive in strategically utilizing local bonds due to the principle of fiscal health and stringent oversight by the central government. For instance, there are significant constraints on borrowing funds from the private sector for public projects, as opposed to using public resources. Consequently, employing local bonds for regional development ranks as the lowest priority in the realm of fiscal policy. Instances of local governments utilizing sources other than public loans or local bond securities(sales bonds) are not common.

In light of changing policy dynamics, strategic considerations regarding local bonds are imperative. With the rising demand for public services and increasingly diverse preferences among residents, the realm of local government services has diversified. This, in turn, signifies a growing demand for local finance.

In addition, it is increasingly challenging for the fiscal capacity of the central government to bear the full burden of various burgeoning physical investment projects. Hence, when central government funding becomes unfeasible, there arises a strategic necessity to activate local bond resources under the autonomous responsibility of local governments.

Therefore, it is necessary to enhance the use of local bonds by aligning them with regional investment projects. As the nature of local government investment projects becomes more detailed, the composition of deployable resources can be planned in an integrated manner. In essence, a strategic approach is needed where local bonds are employed for portions where sufficient revenue can be secured, rather than relying on general resources from the general accounts.

2. Adoption of Specialized Techniques for Management

Systematic fiscal management techniques are essential, as they will diversify the composition of resources related to investment projects. Advanced approaches, such as a sinking fund reserve, a local bond management special account, and digitization of local bonds operation, are necessary.

Local governments have so far primarily managed investment projects centered on general resources. As a result, in terms of fiscal management, they focus solely on monitoring whether the implementation of projects is proceeding as planned according to the performance-to-objective ratio. Indeed, the need for local governments to formulate proactive strategic plans for resource mobilization through a comprehensive review of financial analysis of investment projects was not as significant in the past.

Given the increasing diversification of local government projects and the corresponding multidimensional nature of funding sources provided, there is a growing need to adopt fiscal management techniques tailored to the characteristics of each project and funding source. For instance, a capital budgeting law at the local government level could strategically enable the management of local debt, including local bonds.

3. Governmental Support by the Central Government

Institutional support from the central government is necessary to activate local bonds as a strategic resource for regional development. So far, various regulations and policies from the central government have constrained the use of local bonds by local governments. Given the escalating value of local bonds as a developmental resource, policy and regulatory direction must shift away from passive restraint toward actively providing information and support. Compared with Japan, the acquisition of public funds for funding local bonds in South Korea is insufficient.

It is also necessary to enhance the distribution of various public funds related to local bonds. In this respect, establishing and operating a centralized "local bond acquisition exclusive financial institution" is required. Beyond the limitations of the Regional Development Fund in terms of region and scale, there is a need to use nationally operated funds.

4. Establishment of a Specialized Network

A synergistic network with experts from the private sector who deal with fund procurement should be established. With the expansion of the domestic financial market and increased market activities, various financial products have emerged, offering diverse possibilities for mobilizing funds. Moreover, for executing fund mobilization plans that require specialized knowledge, such as issuing foreign bonds, the support of financial experts becomes crucial. This entails a comprehensive understanding of the various procedures outlined in relevant regulations, insights into trends in the domestic funding market, and knowledge of currency fluctuations in the international funding market. Additionally, a precise analysis of trends in the funding markets of countries subject to government bonds is essential.

Local governments face practical limitations in their fiscal management departments when attempting to grasp such specialized knowledge comprehensively. Moreover, it may not be desirable from a human resource management perspective. Therefore, local governments should strive to establish and use a network for fund management and resource mobilization through organic communication with experts or institutions in the private sector. This approach will facilitate the timely acquisition of reliable information more conveniently.

Chapter 5

Local Fiscal Management System

Section 1 The Purpose of a Fiscal Management System

1. Budget Management Process of Local Governments

Local governments do not manage their budgets independently. Numerous institutional factors directly or indirectly influence local budgets. The local budgeting process is characterized by its integration into the subsector of the central government budget process. Various fiscal expenditure processes of local governments are intricately linked to the comprehensive or individual fiscal plans and projects of the central government.

The local budgeting process originates from the Mid-term Local Finance Plan. It is linked to the local finance impact assessment, feasibility study, and fiscal investment review system in relation to major projects included in the Mid-term Local Finance Plan. In the budgeting process of local governments, information regarding subsidies provided by the central government is crucial.

After budget execution, the post-budget system operated by the Ministry of Interior and Safety becomes operational. Prominent

[Figure 5-1] Budgeting and Fiscal Management Process of Local Governments(Large-Scale Project Example)

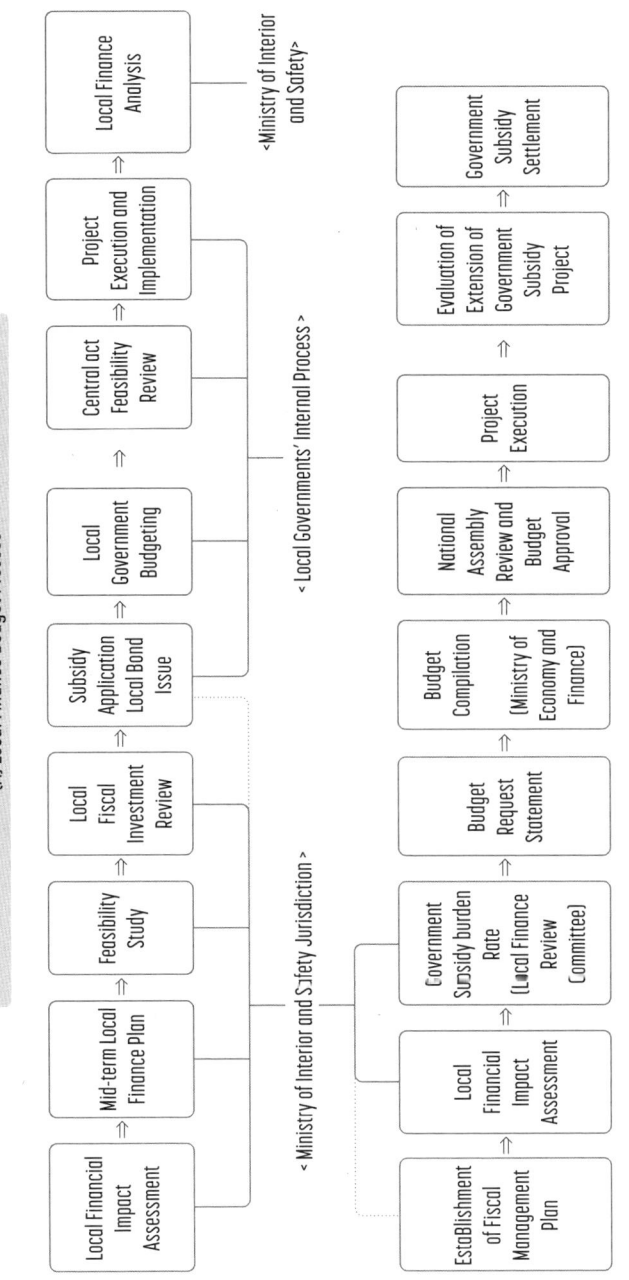

Chapter 5 — · — **Local Fiscal Management System**

instances include the local finance analysis system and the local finance publication system. Principal laws regarding the management of local finances fall under the purview of the Ministry of Interior and Safety, which undertakes a dual function by championing local interests and advocating on their behalf and concurrently controlling local finances from a nationwide standpoint as a central government department.

2. Decentralization and Local Fiscal Management

The institutional management of local taxation began with the enactment of the Local Finance Act in 1963. The key focus here was on the decentralization of authority among central ministries rather than intergovernmental relations. This involved drawing a demarcation line between the budgeting of the Ministry of Home Affairs (local governments) and the control of the Economic Planning Board. Consequently, local finance was liberated from the financial allocation control of the Economic Planning Board at that time. On the other hand, another central ministry overseeing local governments, the Ministry of Home Affairs, still exercised hierarchical control over the expenditure and projects of local governments across the county.

The local fiscal management system outlined in the Local Finance Act started from the functional adjustment of departments in the central government system where local autonomy had not been established. Representative local fiscal management systems operated by the Ministry of Interior and Safety were introduced in the late 1980s. The mid-term local finance plan was introduced in 1988 and the fiscal investment review system in 1994.

Since the revival of local autonomy in 1995, the supervisory functions over local tax-related projects from various central government ministries, including the Ministry of Interior and Safety and the Ministry of Economy and Finance, have been consistently strengthened.

While local governments were previously subordinate administrative bodies of the central government, the transition to a system

<Table 5-1> Cases of Central Operated Local Fiscal Management

	Pre-Fiscal Management	Post-Fiscal Management
Finance Budget Management	Local Governments Budget Compilation Guideline	Local Finance Analysis and Diagnosis
	Mid-term Local Finance Plan	Local Financial Crisis Organizations Designation
	Local Finance Investment Project Review and Feasibility Study	Emergency Fiscal Management Organization Designation
	Government Subsidy Project Guideline(each department)	General Share Tax Reduction Review
	Local Bond Issue Pre-approval (Total amount limit over-issuance)	National Balance Special Account, Local Autonomous Account Assessment Incentives
	New Social Welfare Project Consultation(The Social Security Committee)	Self-evaluation Program for Local Financial Projects (Local Governments)
		Local Finance Publication (local governments)
Policy Management	Local Gender Budget System(Ministry of Interior and Safety, Ministry of Gender Equality and Family)	Ministry of Interior and Safety Joint Assessment (Government Subsidy Projects)
	Gender Impact Assessment System(Ministry of Gender Equality and Family)	Evaluation of Extension of Government Subsidy Project (Ministry of Economy and Finance)
	Participatory Budgeting System(Ministry of Interior and Safety)	Residents' Lawsuits(Ministry of Interior and Safety)

Chapter 5 — · — **Local Fiscal Management System**

of self-government and decentralization necessitated a new form of intergovernmental fiscal relationship. However, this direction did not emphasize local autonomy and responsibility. Instead, it reinforced a hierarchical fiscal management system centered on each ministry within the central government. This resulted in a mismatch between self-government and decentralization in administration and centralization in fiscal management, creating a discordant rhythm between the two aspects.

Section 2 Pre-Budget System

1. The Mid-term Local Finance Plan

The Mid-term Local Finance Plan is a multilayer budget system that reflects the long-term development plans and demands of local governments. It operates as a rolling plan over a five-year period to ensure efficient and systematic local finance management. Since 1988, the Ministry of Interior and Safety has provided a guideline for local governments to operate the plan collectively. They comply with the contents of the plan and report at Cabinet meetings. If projects are not reflected in the plan but are included as budget projects for the following year, the Ministry of Interior and Safety applies substantial punitive measures by reducing the general share tax.

The Ministry of Interior and Safety compiles with the nationwide Mid-term Local Finance Plan through inter-department consultations and reports them to Cabinet in March of the following year. Considering the format and procedures, the plan tends to be written more for the purpose of reporting to Cabinet by the Ministry of Interior and Safety rather than serving as local government's self-contained multi-year budget operational plan.

The Mid-term Local Finance Plan serves as both an autonomous fiscal plan for local governments and as a means of supervision by the central government in the realm of local fiscal management. Unfortunately, since the introduction of this system in South Korea, its role has evolved mainly towards strengthening the central government's control and supervision functions. There is a need for a reform that ensures local autonomy and harnesses the benefits of the multilayer budget system for strategic local government projects.

2. Feasibility Study and Local Financial Impact Assessment

A feasibility study is a prerequisite to a fiscal investment review. Specialized institutions analyze the economic viability(cost-benefit analysis), financial viability(Discounted Cash Flow Method), and the feasibility of the projects for investment. The feasibility study applies to new projects with a total cost exceeding 500 billion KRW. However, projects that have undergone a preliminary feasibility study by the National Finance Act and the Management of Public Institutions Act are exempt from this requirement.

In addition, local governments should undergo a local financial impact assessment conducted by the investment review committee when initiating events or projects with significant financial burdens— such as festivals(costs over 300 million KRW) and open call projects (over 500 million KRW)—or participating in large-scale projects planned by the central government. The local financial impact assessment evaluates the scale of local finance burdens, funding methods, and feasibility.

3. Local Finance Investment Review

Local governments must conduct a Local Finance Investment Review to allocate budgets for large-scale investment projects or specific initiatives such as municipal building constructions or local festivals. Projects exceeding a certain scale are subject to investment review by higher-level local governments or the Ministry of Interior and Safety. Projects

<Table 5-2> Criteria for Eligible Projects in Local Finance Investment Review

		Self-review (each local)		Requested review (Central Regional Government)	
		Regional Government	Local Government	Regional Government Review (Local Government Projects)	Central Review (Regional Government and Local Government Projects)
Resource Composition	In case of the Total Own-source Revenue	4 billion won or more	2 billion won or more		
	Not in Case of the Total Own-source Revenue (Cities of over 1 million)	4 billion won or more 30 billion won below	2 billion won or more 6 billion won below (20 billion won below)	6 billion won or more 30 billion won below (Cities of over 1 million excluded)	Regional Government: 30 billion won or more Local Government: 20 billion won or more
	Construction of Administrative, Cultural, Sports Facilities			2 billion won or more	Regional Government: 4 billion won or more Local Government: 20 billion won or more
Irrelevant to resource composition	Foreign Loan Import Project Foreign Investment Project	0.5 billion won or more 1 billion won below			1 billion won or more
	Marketing Facility	0.5 billion won or more 3 billion won below	0.3 billion won or more 0.5 billion won below	0.5 billion won or more 3 billion won below	3 billion won or more
	Event Projects (performance or festivals)	0.3 billion won or more 3 billion won below	0.1 billion won or more 0.3 billion won below	0.3 billion won or more 3 billion won below	

Source: Ministry of Interior and Safety(2017) "local finance investment project review and feasibility study guideline."

that fail to receive approval in the investment review process cannot be included in the budget for the following year.

The subject of the investment review is determined based on the financial scale. However, projects such as the construction or expansion of local government offices, as well as cultural performances and festivals, are subject to investment review even if their budget sizes are relatively modest. This is because the central government has reinforced its management and control over sectors that have raised concerns about inefficiencies and redundancies in local budgets.

Given the scale and ripple effects of local finance projects, a robust investment review is imperative. However, with the flow of autonomy and decentralization, the investment review needs to evolve in a direction that enhances the management capacity within local governments rather than relying on standardized criteria set by the central government. It is important to explore ways to increase the autonomy and accountability of local governments in the investment review process and its outcomes.

Section 3 Post-Fiscal Management

1. Local Finance Analysis System

The Local Finance Analysis System refers to the post-budget system; it analyzes the health and efficiency of local finance. Local finance analysis has been conducted since the 1990s. In 2010, it was formalized through legislation to establish a more systematic management approach. Under the law, local governments should submit a financial report each year to the central government.

The Ministry of Interior and Safety analyzes each financial report by local governments and should evaluate the level of fiscal risk of each local government. When any fiscal risks are identified, the local finance crisis management committee conducts a review. It can make a fiscal diagnosis, designating a fiscal crisis entity or a local government under financial caution.

The local finance analysis holds significant importance as it evaluates both fiscal health and efficiency. Indicators such as fiscal balance and debt-related metrics are employed to evaluate fiscal health. In addition, revenue and expenditure trends are used to figure out fiscal efficiency. Securing the accountability of local governments, the evaluation assesses legal compliance, efforts in finance publication, and responsiveness to finance analysis.

The current local finance analysis system evaluates the finance of local governments across the county through the lens of the central government. Consequently, it has revealed the limitation of fully acknowledging diversity among local regions. There is a need to revamp the system into a tailored framework that aligns with the specific characteristics of each local government, enhancing the acceptance and utilization of the outcomes of finance analysis.

2. Financial Crisis Management

The Ministry of Interior and Safety operates the local financial crisis pre-alert system to manage local finance health and efficiency. This system involves monitoring key financial indicators of local governments to predict and proactively address potential fiscal crises. The process consists of quarterly monitoring of major financial indicators, documentation analysis, and in-depth diagnosis.

If fiscal analysis and the diagnosis show that the financial conditions of local governments are at risk, the local Financial Crisis Management Committee in the Ministry of Interior and Safety designates the entity as a local financial crisis organization. The designated unit must formulate its budgets based on a fiscal health plan.

Under the further deterioration of the fiscal crisis, the Ministry of Interior and Safety can designate an emergency financial management organization. If a local government's financial conditions meet the following three criteria, it can be designated as an emergency financial management organization:

1. The level of fiscal risk has worsened beyond the standard threshold despite being designated as a financial crisis organization and implementing a fiscal health plan for three years.
2. The local government is unable to pay personnel expenses for more than 30 days.
3. The local government has not made principal or interest payments on debts whose repayment dates have passed for more than 60 days.

Once designated as an emergency financial management organization, the local government must develop an emergency financial management plan and undergo a review of these plans.

Section 4 Subsidy and Local Fiscal Management

1. Political Economy of Subsidies

Subsidies serve as both a source of "local" revenue to ensure the financial stability of local governments and a "central" source of funding that imposes responsibility on local governments in terms of expenditures. While referred to as "subsidies" in terms of revenue, they manifest as "subsidized projects" in terms of expenditures. Consequently, the financial characteristics of revenue and expenditures can be configured differently.

The proportion of subsidies in local finance revenue continues to rise. When formulating their annual budgets and reviewing new investment projects, local governments prioritize considering whether they will receive subsidies from the central government. If unable to secure national funding, local governments find it challenging to plan and execute their own projects. With the increasing number of subsidized projects, the financial autonomy of local governments diminishes. Moreover, as the central government entrusts more projects to local governments through national subsidies, it faces difficulties in managing the outcomes of its own financial projects.

In a decentralized nation where power is shared between the central and local governments, subsidized projects may introduce the principal–agent problem. At the central government level, there is a lack of information regarding actual demand and execution, leading to information asymmetry. Local governments may perceive national subsidies as common resources, potentially leading to the tragedy of the commons. However, strengthening central control could further deteriorate the financial efficiency of local governments.

2. Management of National Subsidies by MOIS

The Ministry of Interior and Safety comprehensively manages local governments' national subsidies based on the Local Finance Act. It serves as an advocate and representative to protect local finance in relation to the government subsidy projects of the Ministry of Economy and Finance and various central government ministries. However, the role of the Ministry of Interior and Safety can be constrained by every department in the central government pursuing government subsidy projects from the perspective of fiscal projects.

As the number and scale of government subsidy projects continue to expand, and various forms of inefficiencies, including benefit fraud, worsen, the Ministry of Interior and Safety has strengthened its management functions for the government subsidy projects by the central government, introducing Article 27 in the Local Finance Act in 2014. Specific laws regarding the national subsidy in the Local Finance Act usually involve consultation and reporting.

There is no authority to enforce measures that directly assist their fiscal burden or compel central governments to take actions favorable to local finance. Despite national subsidies being a significant item in local government revenue budgets as a "local" budget, the central government also views them as expenditure budget resources for each department.

3. Evaluation of Subsidy Project System

The evaluation of government subsidy projects from a financial perspective by the Ministry of Economy and Finance aims to prevent the deterioration of fiscal health due to the increasing trend of such subsidy projects. This assessment focuses on determining whether to maintain or extend the government subsidy projects.

Article 15 of the Subsidy Management Act defines the duration of subsidy projects, excluding those specified by presidential decree, to be within three years. Therefore, the Ministry of Economy and Finance reviewed the necessity for extending government subsidy projects on a three-year basis.

Commencing in 2010, the assessment process for government subsidy projects was revised in 2016, transitioning to the evaluation of the extension of government subsidy projects. The methodology was changed to quantitative assessment(extension of a score of 85 or above). The maximum period for the existence of a subsidy project is three years, and it can be extended through the evaluation. The results are submitted to the National Assembly along with the budget proposal. With the increased prominence of issues related to benefit fraud and fiscal inefficiency arising from redundancy with subsidy projects, the Ministry of Economy and Finance has been continuously enhancing the evaluation and management of these projects.

Chapter 6

Local Public Enterprises

Section 1 The Meaning of Local Public Enterprises

1. Significance of Local Public Enterprises

The "Local Public Enterprises Act" is the legal basis for the operation of local public enterprises. It was enacted in 1969 during times of the centralized developmental administration. The local public enterprises defined in the Local Public Enterprises Act are not limited to specific organizations or corporations. Public projects that meet certain criteria are also included in the classification of local public enterprises. For instance, the water service business is subject to the management regulations of 'local public enterprises' while the Busan Metropolitan City's Water Service Headquarter is an administrative organization of the Busan Metropolitan City government.

    The business domain of local public enterprises is defined in Article 2 of the Local Public Enterprises Act as profitable public-interest projects intended to enhance the welfare of residents. In the management of local public enterprises, a balance between public interest and profitability is crucial, and they are operated primarily based on a self-supporting accounting system. Accordingly, local public enterprises adopt the principle of charging beneficiaries or causative parties for the resources required in local public enterprises. Unlike the general accounting of local governments, they operate based on the enterprise accounting standard with double-entry bookkeeping for budget management and accounting. The Ministry of Interior and Safety discloses information about the status and management conditions of local public enterprises on the internet.

2. Types and Businesses of Local Public Enterprises

Types of Local Public Enterprises

Local public enterprises are categorized into local government-directly operated enterprises and local public corporations and industrial complex corporations. Based on the legal nature of their organizational and personnel structure. The former is an administrative organization of the local government, and its employees belong to the local government. They are subject to the Local Public Enterprises Act because it is deemed appropriate to operate the business they handle through a special account, separate from the general account. Local public corporations and industrial complex corporations. Are independent entities funded by local governments, and their employees are considered private-sector individuals. Both local public corporations and industrial complex corporations. Are special entities with provisions for their establishment and operation specified in the Local Public Enterprises Act.

Article 2 of the Local Public Enterprises Act stipulates the business areas to which local public enterprises apply, which are divided into two types. One is the ten mandatory businesses with the specific criteria set in the enforcement decree of the Local Public Enterprises Act. Both the content and scale criteria of the business must be met. The other type is among the businesses that can generate regular income. Local governments can specify the business targets for the application of the

<Table 6-1> Types and Businesses of Local Public Enterprises

Type		Contents
Type	Local Directly Operated Enterprise	- An organization where the local government sets up public enterprise special accounts to carry out businesses directly, operating accounts independently separated from the general accounts. - The organization and personnel belong to the local government. - Examples: Water supply, sewage, public development, regional development funds, etc.
	Local Public Corporation Public Industrial Complex Corporations.	- An independent corporation in which the local government has invested 50% or more. - Operated separately and independently from the local government body, and the status of its workers is that of civilians
Business	Compulsory Application Business	**[Applied mandatorily if it meets certain criteria specified by the Presidential Decree]** 1. Water supply business (excluding village water supply): Daily production capacity of 15,000 tons or more 2. Industrial water supply: Daily production capacity of 10,000 tons or more 3. Rail business (including urban railway): Possession of 50 or more vehicles 4. Automobile transport business: Possession of 30 or more vehicles 5. Local road business (only toll roads): Road management extension of 50 km or more, 3 or more toll tunnels/bridges 6. Sewage business: Daily processing capacity of 15,000 tons or more (equipped with sewage treatment facilities) 7. Housing business: Housing management area or housing construction area of 100,000 or more 8. Land development: Development area of 100,000 or more 9. Trusteeship of housing(including public welfare facilities specified by the Presidential Decree), land, or public/public buildings 10. Public redevelopment and public reconstruction projects according to the Urban and Residential Environment Improvement Act, Article 2, Clause 2
	Voluntary Application Business	**[Businesses of Local Public Enterprises that can cover 50% of regular expenses with regular income]** 1. Businesses where civilian management participation is difficult, recognized as contributing to the enhancement of residents' welfare, local economic vitality, and promotion of local development 2. Compulsory application target businesses that do not meet the natural application criteria 3. Sports facility business as per the Act on Installation and Use of Sports Facilities 4. Tourism business under the Tourism Promotion Act(excluding travel and casino businesses)

Local Public Enterprises Act through local ordinances.

The Status of Local Public Enterprises Establishment

Ministry of Government Administration and Home Affairs(MOGAHA, current Ministry of Interior and Safety). transferred the authority to establish local public enterprises to local governments as a discretionary matter in 1999. Subsequently, as the establishment of local public enterprises by local governments surged, it was stipulated since 2013 that they must consult with MOGAHA beforehand. However, while its substantive management functions remain limited, the number of local public enterprises continues to increase.

As of 2023, there are 410 local public enterprises. Based on the operating method, local government-directly operated enterprises directly run by local governments account for the largest share with 229. In terms of the type of public enterprise, many are operated as administrative organizations of local governments, such as water supply, sewage, and local development funds. In metropolitan cities, most of the local public enterprises are operated by the city's main office. In regions, there are more local public enterprises in cities and counties than in the regional government office. Most of the local public enterprises in the autonomous districts of metropolitan cities are facility management public corporations. Regionally, Gyeonggi-Province has the highest number of local public enterprises with 105, while in other regions, the number of local public enterprises is less than 40.

Section 2 Financial Situations of Local Public Enterprises

1. Financial Scale of Local Public Enterprises

As of the fiscal year ending in 2022, the financial scale of local public enterprises stands at about 67.1 trillion won. It is incremental although there are fluctuations year by year. The financial scale is concentrated

<Table 6-2> Status of Local Public Enterprises Establishment by Local Gov'ts

(unit: number)

	Regional Government			Local Government			Total
	Direct	Public Corporation	public Industrial Complex Corporation	Direct	Public Corporation	public Industrial Complex Corporation	
Seoul	2	4	2			24	32
Busan	2	3	2			2	9
Daegu	2	2	1			1	6
Incheon	3	3	2			8	16
Gwangju	2	3	1			3	9
Daejeon	2	3	1				6
Ulsan	2	1	1			4	8
Sejong	3	1	1				5
Gyeonggi	2	4		68	24	7	105
Gangwon		1		23	2	6	32
Chungbuk		1		17	1	2	21
Chungnam		1		30	1	4	36
Jeonbuk		1		17	1	1	20
Jeonnam		1		19		1	21
Gyeongbuk		2		28	2	7	39
Gyeongnam		1		27	4	7	39
Jeju	3	3					6
Total	23	35	11	229	35	77	410

Source: Clean Eye System(http://www.cleaneye.go.kr)

<Table 6-3> Financial Scale of Local Public Enterprises(2022)

(unit: 100 million won, %, number)

		2018	2019	2020	2021	2022 size	2022 rate	2022 Number
Direct	Water	86,987	94,999	102,789	98,402	97,550	14.5	122
	Sewer	99,503	108,415	109,496	103,861	104,908	15.6	104
	Public Development	28,806	26,299	32,622	37,850	29,398	4.4	25
	Public Transportation	215	232	205	212	232	0.0	1
	Subtotal	215,511	229,946	245,111	240,325	232,088	34.6	252
Public Corporation	Urban Railway	52,067	48,177	52,589	55,791	61,864	9.2	6
	Urban Development	186,861	227,322	244,439	272,967	274,947	41.0	16
	Others	39,428	41,935	45,181	64,768	65,995	9.8	49
Public Industrial Complex Corporation	Local Public Corporation	26,520	29,280	28,623	34,221	36,418	5.4	96
	Subtotal	304,876	346,714	370,832	427,747	439,224	65.4	167
Total		520,387	576,660	615,944	668,072	671,312	100.0	419

Source: Clean Eye System(http://www.cleaneye.go.kr)

in some public enterprises. Sixteen local public enterprises related to urban development account for 27.5 trillion won, representing 41.0% of the total financial scale. Following that, water and sewage enterprises account for 9.7 trillion won and 10.5 trillion won respectively. Other local public enterprises account for less than 10% of the total scale. Although there are only six urban railway public enterprises, they have a significant financial weight, accounting for 9.2% of the overall financial scale.

2. Financial Soundness of the Local Public Enterprises

The Local Finance Act emphasizes financial prudence as a basic principle of local financial operations. Most local financial outlays have strong characteristics of general administrative management. However, the operation of local public enterprises is an exception to this principle. These enterprises are expected to operate under a balanced approach of profitability and public interest, adopting a self-supporting accounting system. It is realm that necessitates activities of political entrepreneurs within local governments. In the process of such entrepreneural activities, issues regarding financial soundness emerge regularly.

Based on the 2022 financial statements, the debt of local public enterprises amounts to 61.3 trillion won. The urban development sector accounts for a significantly high proportion of this debt, representing 68.5%. This is followed by urban railways at 14.8%, and sewage services at 8.3%. Debt proportions in other sectors are relatively low. The overall debt ratio for local public enterprises stands at 36.0%. However, due to the urban development sector's enterprises having a debt ratio of 164.1%, the overall average is skewed higher. Debt ratios in other sectors are less than 60%.

The Ministry of Interior and Safety operates a separate double-entry bookkeeping special account, distinguished from the general account of local finance, for the soundness of local finance or debt management. The 'Debt Ratio Target System' is a representative measure for debt

<Table 6-4> Debt Scale and Ration of the Local Public Enterprises(2022)

(unit: 100 million won, %)

		2018	2019	2020	2021	2022 size	2022 rate	2022 Number
Direct	Water	6,314	5,534	5,687	8,130	7,850	1.3	2.0
	Sewer	58,942	56,536	53,643	54,060	50,992	8.3	10.4
	Public Development	30,814	15,911	12,700	9,943	7,054	1.2	2.6
	Public Transportation	10	14	16	19	20	0.0	19.0
	Subtotal	96,080	77,995	72,044	72,151	65,916	10.8	36.0
Public Corporation	Urban Railway	67,655	63,242	82,674	88,673	90,583	14.8	42.0
	Urban Development	339,357	356,314	365,797	373,115	420,226	68.5	164.1
	Others	18,524	23,592	22,184	27,244	32,251	5.3	52.4
Public Industrial Complex Corporation	Local Public Corporation	3,154	3,826	3,483	3,871	4,182	0.7	59.9
	Subtotal	428,690	446,974	474,138	492,903	547,242	89.2	101.3
Total		524,770	524,970	546,183	565,055	613,158	100.0	36.0

Source: Clean Eye System(http://www.cleaneye.go.kr)

management. Urban development local public corportations have a debt ratio target of 250%, urban railway local public enterprises 100%, and local corporations established by local governments 200%. Also, when selected as an agency needing focused debt management, they are obliged to establish a financial and debt management plan for five fiscal years annually and disclose the performance externally.

3. Political Economy of Debt and Public Fees

The debt of local public enterprises is determined by various factors such as macroeconomics, policy direction, and public fees. For example, the debt of urban development public enterprises is closely linked to the real estate market and rental housing policy. The debt ratio decreases if the pre-sale rate of various development projects is high, On the other hand, debt accumulates if the economic downturn continues and unsold inventory accumulates. The active operation of rental housing policy also affects the debt ratio.

In the case of urban railways, it is closely related to free rides for the elderly aged 65 and over. The free ride fare policy falls under the realm of elderly welfare policy. The Korea Railroad, a national public enterprise, receives financial support from the central government for fare discounts for the elderly. There is no financial support from the central government for subways in metropolitan cities. The debt of local sewage services public enterprises is intertwined with the issue of actualizing sewage usage fees.

The government sometimes intervenes to prevent increases in local public fees because raising public fees of local public enterprises is related to inflation. The Ministry of Interior and Safety evaluates local governments' efforts to manage public fees in its local price management policy. The Ministry of Economy and Finance also operates the "Local Public Fee Stabilization Incentive System" when distributing resources from the Special Account for Balanced National Development.

<Table 6-5> Local Public Enterprises Management Evaluation Indexes(2023)

Primary Classification	Secondary Classification	Tertiary Classification	Points	
			Qualitative	Quantitative
I Business (63 points)	Leadership (15 points)	1. Management Layers' Leadership	5	
		2. Strategic Management	3	2
		3. Innovative Management	4	1
	Management System (13 points)	1. Organization·Personnel Management	5	
		2. Financial Management	5	3
	Job Creation (6 points)	Job Creation and Work-life balance	4.5	1.5
		Communication and Participation	4	1
	Social Responsibility (29 points)	Ethical Management	5	
		Disaster·Safety Management	5	5
		Regional Co-prosperity and Development	4	5
II Business Performance (40 points)	Major Business Items	Varies depending on the type of business and institution		
	Business Efficiency	Varies depending on the type of business and institution		
	Customer Satisfaction (8 points)	1. Customer Satisfaction	8	
Total(100 points)			50.5	49.5

Note: Different evaluation criteria scores are applied for urban railways and urban development in the area of disaster and safety management.
Source: Ministry of Interior and Safety(2022). 2023 Local Public Enterprises Management Evaluation Guide.

Section 3 Management of Local Public Enterprises

1. Local Public Enterprises Management Evaluation

Since 1993, the Ministry of Interior and Safety has been conducting a management evaluation for local public enterprises. Through numerous system reforms, it operates in a format similar to the Management Evaluation System of Public Institutions run by the Ministry of Economy and Finance. The core of the management evaluation centers on on-site field assessments and quantitative index evaluations. The Ministry of Interior and Safety operates the Evaluation Group on Local Public Enterprises Management annually to ensure the accountability of local public enterprises. Fundamental contents of the management evaluation include management principles, such as enhancing economic efficiency and promoting public interest; achieving management goals; efficiency of operations; social responsibility; and customer services.

Management evaluation indicators can be adjusted in response to changes in national tasks and socio-economic issues. Recent management evaluation indicators have incorporated recovering to the pre-COVID-19 levels, implementing ESG(Environmental, Social, and Governance) management principles, reflecting government policy direction indicators, enhancing citizen participation, and supporting for disaster relief activities. Moreover, due to the diverse characteristics of local public enterprises, the evaluation indicators applied differ by institution. For public enterprises and public corporations, scores of evaluation indicators vary depending on the type of business. Moreover, water and sewage services are biennially evaluated with different evaluation indicators.

2. Management Innovation Issues

Managing Requirements for Establishing Local Public Enterprises

There are increasing demands of local governments to establish subsidiary agencies to proactively address regional economic development issues. However, establishing more local public enterprises than necessary without proven viability can result in fiscal wastes and inefficiency. Given the political and economic characteristics of elected local government leaders, there's also an issue of establishing local public enterprises as a favor or position for specific individuals. Due to limited geographic and population coverage of administrative jurisdictions, proliferation of small local public enterprises in various fields from the outset can lead to inefficiency. In response, the Ministry of Interior and Safety mandates the review of viability before establishing local public enterprises.

Managing Business Domains of Local Public Enterprises

There's a contention regarding the appropriate scope of businesses that local public enterprises can undertake. When local governments diversify their business scope too broadly with profit motives, it can dampen private sector economic activities. Issues not only exist between public and private sectors but also within the public sector regarding overlapping business domains, such as those between central government public enterprises and local public enterprises, or between metropolitan public enterprises and local public enterprises. It's crucial to balance the responsibility to realize proactive public administration with efficient local business administration. The Ministry of Interior and Safety introduced a Real-name Business System for projects above a certain scale (20 billion for metropolitan governments and 10 billion for local governments) and mandated disclosure of project backgrounds, contents, and progress. This system aims to facilitate autonomous business domain management through public disclosure.

Improving the Management Evaluation System

From the perspective of local autonomy, there's debate on whether the central government's evaluation of local public enterprises is justifiable. Evaluating local public enterprises based on nationwide standardized criteria can weaken local government autonomy. There's a risk that the operation of local public enterprises aligns too closely with central politics if the evaluation focus and guidelines change with the political shifts in the central government. Operating conditions for public enterprises vary by region, so applying the same evaluation criteria nationwide might be unrealistic.

Innovating Organization and Financial Management

Local public enterprises or government-funded or contributed local public enterprises often face inefficiencies due to organizational redundancy and lack of economies of scale. There is not much opportunity for local public enterprises to realize economies of scale because their business scope is geographically limited to their jurisdiction. A typical example is local facilities management corporations in autonomous districts. It is less likely to improve efficiency through agreements with neighboring jurisdictions considering the political and economic realities of local autonomy. The rigidity and stagnation may occur in the organizational management if a limited organizational and staffing structure persists for years. It leads to lax management of local public enterprises.

Concerns about debt and fiscal soundness remain important policy area yet the frequency of discussions has diminished. Debt management is particularly crucial for local public enterprises handling urban development, urban railways, and water and sewage services. The debt issues in these three areas vary due to their policy nature, making them structural domains that local public enterprises cannot solve on their own.

Chapter 7

Value Budgeting and Financial Management

Section 1 Participatory Budgeting

1. Significance of Participatory Budgeting

The Local Finance Act Article 39 provides a legal basis for the participatory budgeting system. Initially, the nature of the participatory budgeting was recommendatory when the system was first introduced. Later, the law was amended to make it mandatory and specified the detailed procedures and methods for operating the participatory budgeting system in the law.

Participatory budgeting began with civic groups' budget movements. In the late 1990s, civic movements such as the Taxpayer's Declaration and budget monitoring began. They asked for securing "Taxpayer's Sovereignty" and entailing the right to know the details of government budget expenditures, the right to participate in budget spending decisions, and the right to demand the recovery of wasteful budgets.

2. Introduction of Participatory Budgeting

The participatory budgeting system was first implemented in Porto Alegre, Brazil, in 1989. Participatory budgeting in Eastern Europe and Asian countries expanded as a new social movement along with improving democratic experiences and recommendations from international organizations. In the early 2000s, women's groups, including the "Korean WomenLink," and regional welfare movement groups like "Cheonan Welfare World," initiated promoting the participatory budgeting in local government finances. Later, it emerged as a pledge in the 2002 local elections, and the Civic Group Budget Monitoring Network developed a standard ordinance proposal. In 2004, Gwangju City Buk-Gu first introduced the participatory budgeting system by ordinance, and Ulsan Dong-gu also did so in the same year. The central government included the participatory budgeting system in the Local Decentralization Roadmap in 2003 and added a recommendatory clause to the local government budget compilation guidelines in 2004. In 2005, the Local Finance Act was amended to elevate the legal basis for the participatory budgeting system. In 2011, all local governments were mandated to implement Participatory Budgeting. The "Local Finance Act" and its enforcement decree outline general principles, while specific implementation forms are operated diversely through local ordinances.

3. Issues of Participatory Budgeting

There are high expectations and symbolic achievement associated with the participatory budgeting system when it comes to the value of fiscal democracy and the representativeness and rationality of budget formulation. However, in reality, many challenges still remain. The proportion of the budget directly related to the participatory budgeting system remains low, limiting its actual impact on the

[Figure 7-1] Participatory Budgeting Process of Gwangju City Buk-Gu

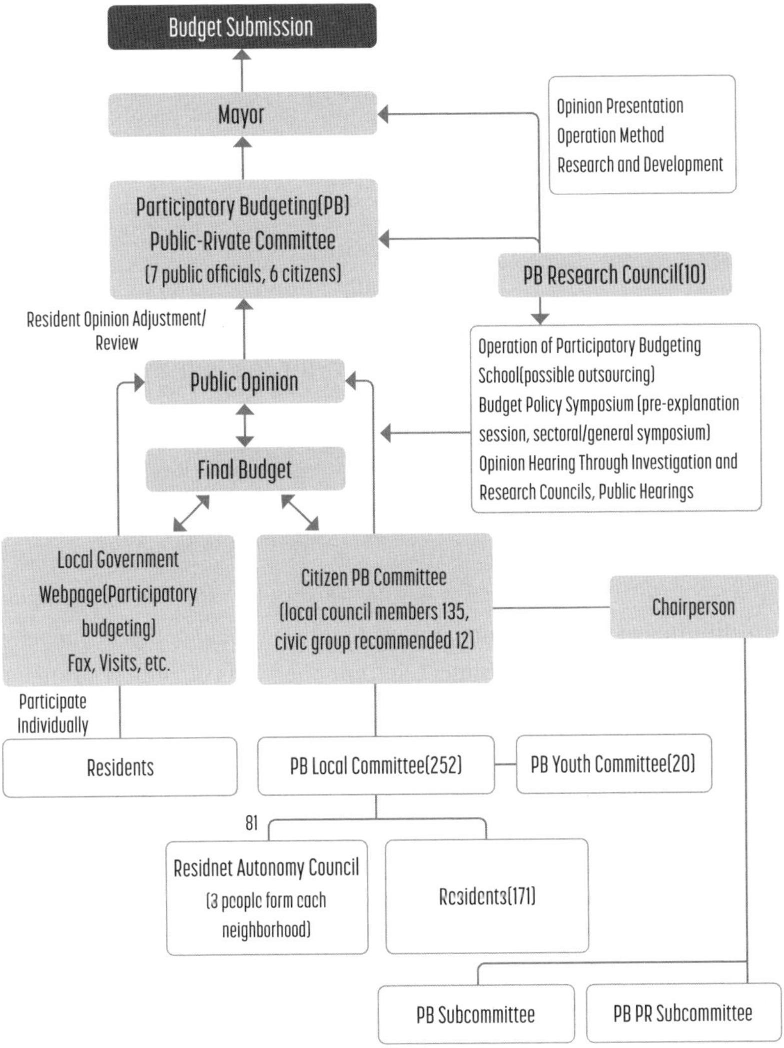

Source : Gwangju City Buk-Gu Webpage(http://bukgu.gwangju.kr)

budget.[01] Therefore, many argue that residents' participation should be institutionalized for major fiscal projects as a whole.

In addition, there's significant criticism from local councils and municipal officials. Local councils criticize that the executive branch weakens the council's exclusive right to budget allocation and adoption. Executive officials worry that participatory budgeting might become a lobbying channel for interest groups or stakeholders. This is because securing the expertise, enthusiasm, and budget neutrality of participating residents is not easy in reality.

Section 2 Local Government Gender Budget System

1. Significance of the Gender Budget System

The gender budget system is a national-level policy tool to implement gender equality. It is linked with gender statistics and gender impact analysis assessment systems. A gender-sensitivity refers to recognizing the differences between men and women in national policies, budgets, and systems. The gender budget system analyzes the budget's impact on women and men from a gender-sensitive perspective, aiming to enhance gender equality in budget formulation and execution. Given that it originated from the feminist movement, a major objective is to expand budget allocations for women in reality.

In local government budgeting and financial management, the gender budget system was implemented in connection with the National Finance Act. When the National Finance Act was enacted in 2007, it mandated the implementation of the gender budget system in central government financial projects from 2010. Later, the 2011 amendment to the Local Finance Act introduced the obligation for local governments

---

01 "The 2018 participatory budgeting of Gwangju Buk-gu Office consists of 95 projects, which is a total of 35.1 billion won. It is only 0.14% of the general account total budget of 5,736 billion won."

to prepare a gender budget statement and settlement statement in Articles 3-2 and 36-2.

The core value of the gender budget is "gender mainstreaming." It aims that a gender perspective should be integrated across all societal domains, not only in women's policy categories but also in general policy areas. The gender budget policy started in 1983 with Australia's "Women's Budget." From the mid-1990s, international organizations like UNDP and UNIFEM recommended the gender budget policy. It was adopted as a code of action at the 1995 Beijing Women's Conference. Since then, many countries have implemented the gender budget system.

2. Main Contents of the Gender Budget Statement

As stipulated in the Local Finance Act, local governments must attach a gender budget statement when they submit a budget proposal to the local council. Also, their settlement statement should include a gender budget settlement. Based on the 2023 original budget, the gender budget statements cover approximately 7.8% of the total local government budget. The proportion of general account projects is significantly high, and many of them are small-and-micro-scale projects.

Gender budget projects must conduct a gender impact assessment based on the gender equality perspective, and the results should be applied to the next year's budget. Projects such as the Basic Plan on Gender Equality and Gender Impact Analysis, both overseen by the Ministry of Gender Equality and Family, are all included in the gender budget. In addition, financial projects conducted by local governments for gender equality are included at their discretion.

The gender budget statement includes information on the gender-oriented allocation of budget resources, distinguishing between male and female beneficiaries, and information on performance targets for that year. For programs with many female beneficiaries, performance targets might use indicators to increase male participation or the male beneficiary rate.

<Table 7-1> Scale of Local Government Gender Budget Items(2023)

(unit: 100 millions won, %)

		N of Projects	Budget	Proportion(%)	Note
Projects Related to the Basic Plan on Gender Equality	General Account	4,318	63,061	26.6	Subsidized or Autonomous Projects Related to The 2nd Basic Plan on Gender Equality
	Other Special Account	14	377	0.2	
	Subtotal	4,332	63,438	26.7	
Projects related to the Gender Impact Analysis	General Account	10,239	108,894	45.8	Projects under the Gender Impact Analysis and Evaluation Act
	Other Special Account	144	4,120	1.7	
	Subtotal	10,383	113,014	47.6	
Local Government Projects	General Account	2,431	60,411	25.4	Projects Conducted by Local Governments for Gender Equality
	Other Special Account	37	643	0.3	
	Subtotal	2,468	61,054	25.7	
Total		17,183	237,506	100.0	7.8% of Total Budget

Source: Ministry of Interior and Safety(2023). Integrated Financial Summary of Local Governments 2023.

3. Issues of the Gender Budget System

Even after a considerable period has passed since the introduction of the gender budget system, it has not settled as a universal value budget in local finance. While the name of gender budget includes the term "budget," the gender budget statement is not a legal document but a "report." There are limitations in ensuring the practicality of expanding the women's budget or enhancing gender equality because the gender budget statement is just a supplementary document attached to the budget proposal. The number of projects and the scale of the budget included in the local government gender budget are increasing every year; however the expected effects and results on gender equality are limited.

In addition, there are instances where the gender budget projects conflict with the principles of existing budget projects, making it challenging to overcome the path dependency barriers of budget projects. There is also a tendency that the gender budgets are limited to residual social welfare policies. When the residual nature of welfare policies overlaps with the residual nature of women's policies, it is challenging to operate them as mainstream budget's financial projects.

The gender budget system is similar with the participatory budgeting system in that both are originated from civic movements. Both of them have elements that are hard to coexist with traditional budgeting practices. However, differences exist in the perspective of the local government budgeting and financial management innovation particularly for the decentralization initiatives and the spontaneity of local governments. Participatory Budgeting started in Gwangju Buk-gu and spread to other local governments, and then spread nationwide through the Local Finance Act. It underwent a bottom-up diffusion process starting from the local level.

In contrast, the gender budget system was institutionalized during the political negotiation process when reforming the (former) Budget and Accounting Act of 2007 to the (current) National Finance Act. The central budget department tends to be passive about this system, which is a product of political negotiations. Linked to the National Finance Act, the local government gender budget was newly established during the 2011 Local Finance Act revision. It's a local budget system that underwent a top-down diffusion process starting from the Ministry of Economy and Finance. Consequently, from the beginning, the Ministry of Interior and Safety and local government budget departments were passive. They applied the central government's budget framework directly to the local level. The awareness and participation of local civil society organizations, central departments, and local executive departments have not been as active as expected.

Section 3 Local Grant Budget Management

1. Significance of Local Grant

The term "local grant" is a legal term found in actual laws. It is a term that integrates both the civil transition subsidies that local governments provided free of charge to projects autonomously carried out by individuals or private corporations, and the fiscal subsidies that metropolitan governments support basic local governments with based on policy needs.

Local grants are resources without any quid pro quo that foster and support specific activities of individuals and groups within the region. They are distinct from compensatory expenses like private trust money, which specifies certain activities, or interest subsidies. Designing a standard management system is not easy because the targets of subsidy support are quite varied, and regional characteristics are also different. Considering the political and economic environment of a region, grant supports get hard to terminate once support starts for specific organizations or individuals.

2. Local Grant Budget and Management

The local grant organizes the business expenses related to the tasks of local governments as a budget. Except in cases with explicit legal grounds, it cannot be allocated for operational purposes. The amount for the local grant should be determined considering the nature of the supported project, the ability of the supporter to bear the cost, and must be organized by project within the scope reviewed by the "Local Grant Review Committee."

Each local government has a total limit for local grants. This total limit is set considering the average increase/decrease rate of general account own-source revenue over the past three years based on the budget size of the previous year. Grant budget should systematically manage various information such as support history to prevent local grants from being granted with overlapping or granted to ineligible individuals. Local governments must conduct performance evaluations annually and reflect the results in the budget. For ongoing grant projects, the need for continuation should be evaluated every three years, and measures should be taken based on the evaluation results after review by the "Local Grant Review Committee."

3. Issues in Managing the Local Grant Budget

The local grant management system became a focal point because financial supports from local governments to regional civic society organizations has expanded. Accounting management of civic organizations, which were not included in the public expenditure management system, is evaluated as loose and opaque from the perspective of public management.

The Ministry of Interior and Safety and local governments continuously strengthened the local grant management system to enhance the transparency and efficiency of public resources. However, from the viewpoint of value budgeting, there are three latent issues:

First, local grants for regional civic society organizations serve as incentive resources for citizen participation and the activation of a co-production partnership system for local public services. But if the administrative and financial management capabilities of the support organizations are insufficient or they prefer not to be included in the official financial management system, there's a risk that a privilege cartel centered on specific organizations will form. A balance between promoting co-production partnership and strengthening the public financial management of public resources is needed.

Second, civic organizations fundamentally operate as non-profit organizations and have high financial flexibility. If local grants and the self-expenses of regional civic organizations mix, financial rigidity can occur, making the expected flexibility and cost-effectiveness in a co-production system vulnerable.

Third, strengthening local grant management results in additional administrative expenses related to financial management. Since local support projects in the social service sector are labor-intensive, a significant amount of administrative management costs are incurred. If the allowable range of accounting expenses related to subsidy management expands, the financial expenditure burden of local governments may increase. There's also a risk of reducing the cost-effectiveness through co-production and the innovative effects of public services through a cooperation system with regional civic organizations.

Chapter 8

Social Welfare and Local Finance

Section 1 Welfare Decentralization and Local Finance

1. Local Finance and Social Welfare Expenditure

Social welfare expenses account for more than 30% of local expenditures, and this proportion is expected to increase for the foreseeable future. To secure an appropriate level of available budget through the acquisition of sustainable revenue sources and manage the efficiency, integrity, and responsibility of local finance expenditures, it's crucial to understand the relationship between social welfare and local finance.

Traditionally, social welfare was perceived as the domain of the central government. This concept was established as fiscal federalism in the study of finance for the American welfare state. Since the 1980s, the burden of welfare expenditures on local governments in the West has surged. This disparity between theory and reality occurred due to two factors simultaneously influencing the situation. The primary reason is the financial crisis of or financial pressure from the central government. The central government responded to this fiscal difficulties by reducing welfare programs and transferring welfare expenditure requirements to local governments.

Another significant reason was the expansion of social services in response to new social risks due to the dissolution of families and communities. Tailored local-level and individual-level approaches in various care services and local community services were essential. The financial consequences of local governments' proactive community policies were evident in the increased local welfare expenditures.

In the basic welfare program, which is part of the social safety net, local governments play a secondary role. There lies an inherent conflict of mandatory local contributions to centrally aimed financial projects. In contrast, various social services ensuring daily life in the community are characterized by investments where local governments play the leading role.

In reality, there's considerable fiscal conflict between governments because of the blurred distinction between the two aforementioned approaches in welfare projects. Local governments are marginalized, unable to actively intervene in the social welfare sector, which dominates their expenditures. Structural issues with local welfare finance arise because the boundary of local governments' proactive roles and responsibilities is not clear in the most significant area of expenditure.

2. Local Finance as the Main Player in Welfare Policy

There are three types of social welfare policies advanced by fiscal projects. The Type I projects, covering income and health insurance areas, operate based on a national burden directly managed by the central government through a national social insurance system.

The Type II and Type III proejcts are operated by the local governments as frontline agencies through inter-governmental fiscal relations, utilizing national subsidies. The Type II projects pertain to the realm of the basic welfare program within the social safety net. The

<Table 8-1> Three Types of Social Policy and Policy Governance System

	Purpose	Basic Theory	Welfare Policy	Organizational Structure	Financial Management	Operational Principle	Social Legitimacy
Type I	Income Security Health Security	Welfare State Fordism	National Pension Health Insurance	Public Organization Nationwide Organization	National Charge Social Security Tax	Individual Responsibility Mandatory Membership	Individual Failure
Type II	National Basic Living Security	Relative Poverty Social Safety Net	Basic Security Residual Welfare	Local Government Delegated Affairs	General Account National Subsidies	Income Distribution National Standard Residual Selectiveism	Market Failure
Type III	Societal Basic Daily Life	Social Development Social Investment	Universal Social Service	Performance Contract Collaborative Governance	Welfare Decentralization Comprehensive Assistance	Diversity and Universality Consumer Centric	Societal Failure

Type III projects represent social service fiscal projects, where local finance becomes the principal actor in welfare policy.

Social services addressing new social risks like family and community dissolution require tailored solutions for each region and individual. The standardized project designs and operations of the central government are cost-inefficient. The ideal governance for implementing custom-fit solutions involves decentralization and marketization. In the West, including Europe, the shift towards decentralization and marketization in social welfare service provision is a common trend when promoting the expansion of care services.

Fiscal conflicts between central and local governments regarding social welfare expenditures occur because the governance for the third type projects is not well-established. Undertaking the Type III projects within the foundational welfare system of the Type II project provision leads to continuous increases in social welfare expenditures and a fixation on inefficient fiscal project operations.

3. Welfare Decentralization and Local Finance

Universal social services have a fiscal characteristic where resources are collectively mobilized in the community, resulting in specific individuals having exclusive ownership of those resources. In such cases, the approach should be based on the perspective of resource allocation, such as human capital, social investment, social capital, and social wages, rather than income distribution. When considering the fiscal role of the government, efficiency in resource allocation is closely related to local finance.

Social services that substitute for the functions of families and communities, such as care services, need to be distinguished from traditional social welfare. These areas require a more proactive role from local governments rather than the central government. Even at the micro-level project management, the role of local finance is emphasized. This is primarily because social services need to be supplied variably at

<Table 8-2> Three Types of Social Policy and Policy Governance System

	Welfare Policy	Fiscal Function	Basic Value	Intergovernmental Relations	Notes
Type I	National Pension Health Insurance	Economic Stability	Stability and Balance	The 3rd Institution (Central Governmental public corporation)	Individual-Level Current-Future Consumption/Income Balance
Type II	Baisc Security Residual Welfare	Income Distribution	Social Equity Social Justice	Central Government	Compensating for Market Failure Conflict Mediation between Social Classes
Type III	Universal Social Service	Resource Allocation	Social Efficiency Social Production	Local Government	Sustainable Growth through Social and Economic Integration Restoration Of family Functioning and Community

Chapter 8 — · — **Social Welfare and Local Finance**

the local level. Policy tools also need to be designed considering cost-effectiveness, incorporating various combinations such as cash, in-kind contributions, and vouchers.

Section 2 Issues of Local Social Welfare Expenditure

1. Status of Welfare Expenditure in Local Finance

Rapid Increase in Social Welfare Expenses

Within the classification of local government expenditures by function, social welfare expenses account for about 30% of the total expenditure and continue to increase annually. The characteristics of social welfare expenses in local finance can be summarized as having a large scale and proportion, consistent growth, national subsidy projects and sharing mandatory, pressure on local finances and distortion in the local financial system, and vulnerability in solving community issues.

Based on the 2023 original budget, social welfare costs account for 31.5%, totaling 96.3 trillion won. Excluding social welfare costs, the spending proportion of other fiscal functions is all below 10%. This is not due to the local government's autonomous or discretionary spending increase. It's because of the mandatory linkage of local finance caused by the central government's increase in subsidy project costs.

Since 2007, universal social services like the Social Service E-Voucher program began to expand from the perspective of social investment policy. The size of local finance spending increased by 2.2 times in 2023 compared to 2010. During the same period, social welfare costs surged by a high rate of 3.6 times. The proportion of social welfare costs in local finance was 19.0% in 2010 and increased to 31.5% in 2023, which was 12.5 percentage points increase.

<Table 8-3> Changes in the Proportion of Local Expenditures by Function

(Unit: 100 mil KRW, %)

		Proportion							Scale	
		2010	2023	Total	2023 Expenses				2010	2013
					Policy Projects		Operational Cost	Fiscal Activities		
					Subsidized	Own				
General Administration	General Administration	8.6	5.4	100.0	7.2	73.4	-	19.5	119,620	166,085
	Public Safety	1.6	1.9	100.0	32.5	48.6		18.9	21,758	58,567
	Sub-otal	10.1	7.4	100.0	13.8	66.9		19.3	141,378	224,652
Social Development	Education	5.8	5.3	100.0	4.3	95.1	-	0.6	81,385	161,885
	Culture and Tourism	5.6	4.7	100.0	38.0	60.0		2.0	77,949	142,778
	Environmental Protection	10.7	9.6	100.0	39.9	56.9		3.1	149,026	293,022
	Social Welfare	19.0	31.5	100.0	89.6	9.7		0.8	265,342	963,192
	Public Health	1.6	1.8	100.0	72.6	27.2		0.2	22,250	53,674
	Subtotal	42.6	52.9	100.0	66.9	31.8		1.3	595,952	1,614,551
Regional Development	Agriculture Marine Fishery	7.0	6.7	100.0	66.7	32.3		1.0	97,237	203,672
	Industry and SME	2.2	2.7	100.0	40.2	53.6		6.2	30,172	83,313
	Traffic and Logistics	11.8	8.1	100.0	27.2	65.0		7.8	164,648	246,100
	Land and Regional Development	9.2	5.6	100.0	28.9	60.8		10.2	128,440	171,657
	R&D	0.3	0.1	100.0	26.1	72.6		1.3	4,375	3,825
	Subtctal	30.4	23.2	100.0	40.5	53.3		6.2	424,872	708,567
	Reserve Funds, etc	16.9	16.6	100.0	0.1	22.5	76.7	0.7	236,364	506,337
	Total	100.0	100.0	100.0	45.8	37.9	12.7	3.6	1,398,566	3,054,107

Note: General and Special Accounts Original budget net total
Source: MOIS(each year). *Local Government Integrated Financial Overview(top)*.

Welfare Spending Centered on National Subsidy Projects

Each year, approximately 90% of local social welfare costs are subsidy projects. It means that the proportion of the local government's own-sourced welfare project costs is merely about 10%. Since the 2000s, the focus on social welfare in local finances has been to carry out the central government's national subsidy projects. The performance of own-sourced welfare projects by local governments is very limited, except for a few local governments. The central government also has a tendency to suppress the advancement of own-sourced welfare projects by local governments. It became mandatory to consult with the central government regarding own-sourced projects, and also established guidelines that impose financial penalties when cash benefit welfare spending is excessive.

Local Welfare Financial Burden Centered on Basic Welfare Programs

Welfare subsidies are concentrated in large-scale cash benefits projects and large social service projects that have limited financial discretion. As a result, local governments are unable to secure discretion in expenditure management. They are compelled to share local costs mandatorily for central government projects, pressuring them to mobilize their own resources. For policies like the basic pension, if the expenditure size increases step-by-step according to the political election cycle, an unexpected rise in local costs occurs in the medium term, irrespective of local financial conditions.

Based on the 2022 original budget, the financial scale of the eight major welfare projects operated by the Ministry of Health and Welfare is 51.0 trillion won. This accounts for 57.8% of the 88.1 trillion won in local government social welfare costs. The financial expenditure scale of the major welfare subsidy projects is institutionally determined according to relevant laws, irrespective of the national or local financial conditions. Overall, the national subsidy rate is high at 75.7%. However, centered on cash benefits welfare projects, the expenditure scale for each project is determined at a level that exceeds the growth rate of

<Table 8-4> Basic Welfare Program in Local Welfare Costs(2022)

(Unit: 100 mil. KRW, %)

		Total Cost	National Cost	Local Cost	Natinoal Subsidy Rate
Basic Livelihood Security	Living Security Benefit	63,345	52,611	10,734	83.1
	Medical Security Benefit	102,634	77,013	25,621	75.0
Support for the Vulnerable	support for activities for the disabled	26,193	17,405	8,788	66.5
	disability pension	12,406	8,322	4,084	67.1
Elder·Youth	basic pension	198,712	159,991	38,722	80.5
	Senior Employment and Social Activities Program	28,844	14,422	14,422	50.0
Child Care·Family and Women	Child Care Allowance	31,557	24,035	7,522	76.2
	Childcare Subsidies	45,861	32,027	13,834	69.8
	Total	509,552	385,826	123,727	75.7

Note: 2022 original budget
Source: Korea Fiscal Information Service e-Naradoum(https://opn.gosims.go.kr)

local general revenue, significantly pressuring the local finance's share of welfare costs.

2. Issues in and Inter-Governmental Welfare Finance

Welfare Subsidies and Pressure on Local Finance

The resources for local government welfare projects are mostly composed of national and local costs. Over the past decade, the annual growth rate of local general resources from local taxes and the growth rate of welfare subsidies have been inconsistent, with significant fluctuations year by year. This makes it challenging to maintain the stability of local finance.

Regardless of the local government fiscal conditions, welfare subsidy projects were promoted according to the central government's policy direction. Over a decade, the annual growth rate of welfare subsidies exceeded the growth rate of local government general revenue. In 2021, the growth rate of local government general revenue was a mere 1%, while welfare subsidies increased by 8.7%.

Region-Local Welfare Financial Relationship

Autonomous urban districts face significant financial strain due to welfare costs. Based on the 2023 original budget, the nationwide net scale of social welfare costs is 96.3 trillion won, of which autonomous districts spend 25.9 trillion won, accounting for 26.9%. Autonomous districts allocate 56.0% of their expenditure budget to welfare projects, and there's a notable disparity among districts. The proportion of social welfare costs in Busan's Buk-gu is 71.4%, the highest in the nation. Since the revival of local autonomy in 1995, the administrative and financial systems that were centralized at the time have remained entrenched, continuing without significant changes to date

However, unlike the significance of the proportion of social welfare costs in the autonomous district budget, the scale and proportion of autonomous district expenses in the funding structure for district welfare projects are not relatively large. Based on the 2022 original budget, the district's share in the social welfare cost funding structure is about 14.5%. In the case of Busan, district expenses account for only 3% in over 480 national welfare-related subsidized projects. Considering the funding structure and the share of district social welfare costs, the cause of the financial pressure on district welfare funding lies more in the vulnerability of the local tax revenue structure of the district than

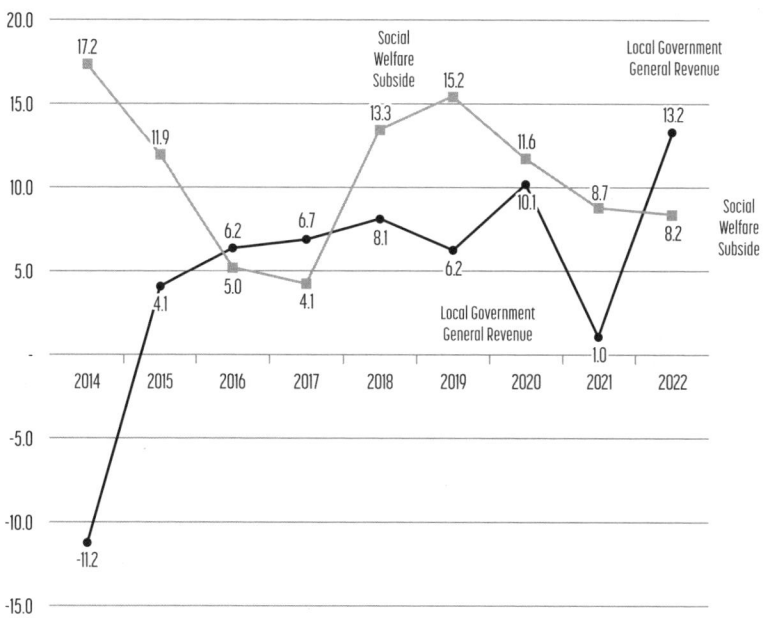

[Figure 8-1] Trend of Local government General Revenue and Welfare Subsidy Increase Rate Change

Note: Local Government General Revenue – Local Tax+Non-tax Revenue+Local Subsidy Tax
Source: MOIS(Each year). *Local Government Integrated Financial Overview(top)*.

in the funding structure itself.

Inefficient & Centralized Project Management System

The social welfare delivery system has limitations in increasing efficiency for the welfare subsidy projects. A lot of costs are incurred in the long delivery system from the central government to the frontline of welfare service provision, and in some cases, fiscal spending does not directly lead to solving social problems. This is due to the characteristics

<Table 8-5> Revenue Sources of Autonomous District Social Welfare Cost(2023)

(Unit: 100 mil. KRW, %)

	Scale				Proportion			
	Total	National Cost	City Cost	District Cost	Total	National Cost	City Cost	District Cost
Seoul Special City	114,981	57,023	32,900	25,058	100.0	49.6	28.6	21.8
Metropolitan Cities	171,082	114,918	39,969	16,195	100.0	67.2	23.4	9.5
Total	286,063	171,941	72,869	41,253	100.0	60.1	25.5	14.4

Note: General Account + Speical Account original budget net total
Source: MOIS(2023). *Local Government Integrated Financial Overview*(top).

of the inter-governmental welfare relationship in the welfare-centric regime. A long delivery system is formed from the central-regional-local-(Intermediate management organization)-beneficiary within centralized vertical national-local relationship. Since welfare projects are operated within the administrative jurisdiction of local governments, there are restrictions on user choices, and it's hard to achieve economies of scale in project management.

In a vertically centralized welfare administrative system with each department of the central government at its pinnacle, it's challenging to ensure efficient innovation in the social service delivery system or cost-effectiveness of social welfare expenses. The inefficiency of national subsidies causes information disparity and moral hazard, leading to weak responsibility points in solving social problems. There's also the issue of quadruple losses due to monopolization as the delivery system monopolizes based on the scale of the jurisdiction of local governments.

While the socio-economic activities of local residents are regionalized beyond the jurisdiction of the basic unit, the social service delivery system operates at the existing local level. Even if there are cases where regional social service solidarity or integrated operation of similar social services is efficient, it's not easy to achieve efficiency or productivity innovation in the field without administrative reforms at the level of the central government's departments.

Section 3 Reform Tasks for Welfare Finance

1. Guaranteeing Local General Revenue

While the central government's welfare expansion policy continues, most welfare subsidy programs are operated with matching funds from the national and local budgets. It is necessary to seek a post-financial correction method through the welfare subsidy guideline system and local financial adjustment system that enforces the growth rates of welfare subsidies and local government general revenue to match.

When setting financial standards, there are ways to set them based on local revenue standards or expenditure standards. For example, from the former perspective, the growth rate of general revenue and the growth rate of revenue sources are important. From the latter's expenditure perspective, the proportion of policy budgets in local finances can be considered. From a financial perspective, it is necessary to limit the scope of conflict points by setting the subsidy guideline business area limited to representative subsidiary businesses (e.g., livelihood allowance, medical allowance, basic pension, childcare support, Child Care Allowance) that have significant cost-effectiveness, rigidity or influential power.

2. Reorganization of the Standard Subsidy Rate

Standard Subsidy Rate Modification

Central government-operated various types of welfare subsidy projects should be classified by financial characteristics and consistently reorganized. A comprehensive modification of the standard subsidy rates for various welfare subsidiary projects presented in the table of the Enforcement Decree of the Subsidy Management Act under the jurisdiction of the Ministry of Economy and Finance is needed.

For example, the standard subsidy rates for livelihood allowance related to income security and disability pension are 80% and 70% respectively. Those for elderly jobs and comprehensive elderly care as social services for living security are 50% and 70%, respectively. It's essential to categorize welfare features into income, health, and life security and differentiate between basic welfare services and additional social services to modify the standard subsidy rate system.

Re-establishment of the Differential Subsidy Ratio System

The differential subsidy ratio system applied to welfare subsidy projects needs an overall overhaul. Many subsidiary projects set a low subsidy rate only for Seoul, stuck in the situation of the mid-1980s. By applying the logic of that time, the metropolitan municipalities should consistently apply the same subsidy rate.

The differential subsidy ratio system for basic welfare programs is no longer useful. Most local governments apply an increased subsidy ratio. It is necessary to abolish the differential subsidy ratio applied to basic livelihood benefits and basic pensions and reform it by raising the standard subsidy rate.

3. Establishment of the Next-Generation System

Central Government Administrative Reform

The three-level delivery path of the central-regional-local leads to redundancy, lack of responsibility, inefficient customs, and excessive administrative costs. There's a need for comprehensive planning, execution, and evaluation of cash-type welfare subsidiary projects under the supervision and control of the central government. The intergovernmental joint fund-sharing is an inefficient financial system where redundant administrative management intervenes in the three-level administrative agencies of central-regional-local.

There's a severe overlap of administrative tasks more than necessary in cash benefits. Considering this, a nation-wide management and operation system for cash benefits, tentatively named the Social Security Agency, could be established. It would be worthwhile to consider selecting and managing beneficiaries uniformly using the computer data of Hangbok e-um and National Pension Management Service.

Reform of the Welfare Financial Operation System

In the financial relationship between the headquarters of the metropolitan city and the autonomous districts, there are issues of information gap and moral hazard. Considering the geographical characteristics of the autonomous district's jurisdiction, a financial structure that inevitably has financial externality due to welfare finance pressure is established. Operating a subsidiary project based on the administrative unit of the autonomous district on the 1/n basis is not cost-effective considering the daily separation of residence and work of citizens and geographical mobility from the user's perspective. A structural reform of the financial relationship between metropolitan and basic in welfare subsidiary business is needed.

First, the scope of projects directly managed by the metropolitan city government, rather than delegating the management of welfare assistance projects to the autonomous districts, should be expanded. Second, it is necessary to modify the fiscal roles of the district adjustment grants and regional assistance funds. It needs to ensure the expenses for the district's welfare assistance projects by strengthening the linkage between the growth rate of financial demand related to social welfare in the metropolitan city's general local tax and the fiscal adjustment system between the metropolitan and local units. Third, the monopolistic assistance project operating system, set within the local government jurisdictions, needs to be reformed. Even under the current administrative units, forming a social service solidarity system that shares the use of welfare facilities through agreements between districts can reduce the inefficiency of monopolies.

Central-Local Welfare Grand Compromise

The current intergovernmental financial relationship is fixed in a structure where the central government takes full responsibility for problem-solving. Accumulated problems of excessive burden and lack of capacity in the social sector by the central government exist fundamentally. The aim is to clearly define the "principle" in the welfare subsidiary projects and eliminate the information gap between the principle and the agents through the Intergovernmental Welfare Grand Compromise.

The proposal is to convert basic welfare programs to national affairs and transfer diverse local social services like infant care to the local level. It is reasonable to convert cash benefits-type basic welfare programs, such as livelihood allowance, medical allowance (integrated with health insurance), basic pension (integrated with National Pension), and disability pension, into national affairs of the central government. It is beneficial for both central and local that it can secure efficiency in project operation methods and content from the management perspective even if the transition of national affairs of government subsidy projects and local transfers is promoted without changing the burden of resources based on the current standards by applying the financial neutrality principle.

It is justified to guarantee basic welfare for all citizens regardless of local financial conditions from the principle of geographical justice. "Information" on cash benefits is more aggregated in the "Hangbok e-um" system of the Ministry of Health and Welfare than in the local government, and the operation of cash payment tasks is more efficient in the national administrative system operated by the National Pension Service or National Health Insurance Service by building a nation-wide welfare banking system.

Chapter 9

Fiscal Decentralization and Intergovernmental Relations

Section 1 Significance of Fiscal Decentralization

1. Meaning of Decentralization and Fiscal Decentralization

Context of Decentralization and Fiscal Decentralization

Fiscal decentralization refers to the transfer of financial authority and functions from the central government to local governments. Financial authority involves reducing the central government's role in areas such as revenue, expenditure, and financial management. Specifically, it includes measures to expand the functions and authority of local governments in areas such as the allocation of tax revenues, discretion over transfer revenues, control over local transfers in fiscal projects, management of aid projects, and oversight of financial operations.

Fiscal decentralization's socio-economic context extends beyond the realm of "finance." It encompasses political aspects related to the separation of powers, democratic elements involving citizen participation, and economic considerations concerning resource allocation and fiscal project efficiency.

In advanced welfare states, Fiscal decentralization was initially a critique of Keynesian political-economic systems. Advocates of fiscal decentralization, based on the Tiebout Hypothesis and public choice theory, argued for its efficiency in decentralization, especially when the central government's fiscal role expanded, particularly in the context of Social Welfare Policy. During the fiscal crisis of the 1980s in welfare states, fiscal decentralization was established as a pragmatic solution under the concept of Government Innovation. It involved transferring welfare financing from the central government to local governments and delegating authority over individual fiscal projects—a method that involved an exchange of resources and authority.

In developed countries where self-government and decentralization principles are well-established, the context of fiscal decentralization differs from that in developing countries. In developing nations, Fiscal decentralization serves as a means of political democratization. Local governance is critical for restructuring centralized power relations, and fiscal decentralization is discussed as a prerequisite for self-governance. In cases where the central government is reluctant to transfer significant authority over fiscal matters, it may actually strengthen local government financial management while expanding self-government and decentralization. The separate pursuit of self-government and decentralization and fiscal decentralization can lead to arbitrary tensions and synergies, with the interplay of institutional arrangements and historical contextual factors related to self-government and decentralization playing a complex role in intergovernmental relations.

2. Three Theoris about Fiscal Decentralization

Intergovernmental relations take various forms depending on historical and situational factors, and the models of specific countries tend to evolve uniquely over time. When the values of self-government and decentralization are integrated into the institutional framework of "nation-local government," there can be a significant mismatch between theoretical discussions and practical realities regarding intergovernmental relations.

At the theoretical level, there are three representative models that serve as the basic frameworks for intergovernmental relations, with the United States, the United Kingdom, and Japan as key examples(Lee, et al., 2014: 418).

Firstly, the Federal Model is based on the historical characteristics of the United States. The term "inter-governmental relations" was first used by C.F. Snider in 1937 in the *American Political Science Review*. Subsequently, in the 1970s, during research activities on the relationship between the central and local governments in federal states, D.S. Wright established it as an academic term. In this model, the federal system is subdivided into independent, cooperative, and overlapping relationships between the central and local governments.

[Figure 9-1] Wright's Model of Inter-governmental Relations

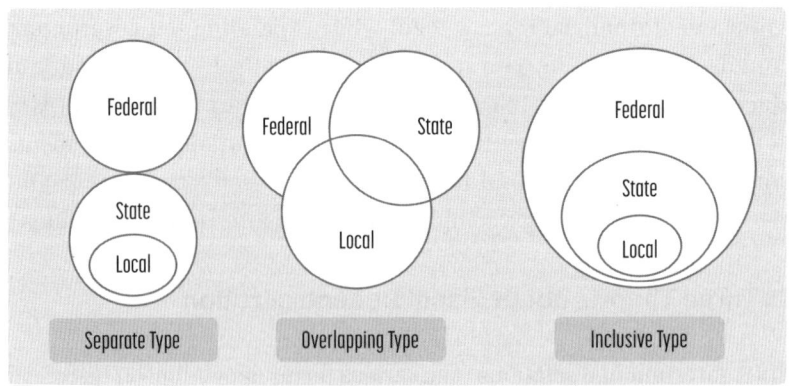

Secondly, there is the UK-style model, where central and local governments are interdependent(Rhodes, 1997). The central government in this model has strong control over local governments, but there is substantial interdependence between them.

Thirdly, there are cases where central and local governments form a hierarchical supervisory system. Japan is a typical example of this, and South Korea also falls into a similar model by applying post-war local autonomy-related institutions from Japan.

In South Korea, local governments are legally considered "organizations" established according to central government laws, which means they have the legal characteristics of subordinate agencies that must faithfully execute legal matters determined by the central government. However, after World War II, Japan's decentralization system, which emphasized the financial independence of local governments, had a significant influence. As a result, South Korea's system and values in local finance have characteristics similar to the federal government relationships in the United States. The system not only includes vertical administrative supervision but also harbors demands and expectations for local autonomy and decentralization innovation within intergovernmental relations-related institutions.

The philosophical basis for the social movement regarding self-government and decentralization heavily relies on European communitarianism. The principle of local governance centered around local government, according to the Principle of Subsidiarity in intergovernmental affairs coordination, has been established. This principle is also reflected in South Korea's Local Autonomy Act. However, during the 1990s, when globalization and government innovation based on global standards were promoted vigorously in South Korea, intergovernmental fiscal relations were significantly influenced by the Fiscal Federalism theory established in the United States. Concepts such as small government, the fiscal functions of government, and the optimal subsidy rate were prominent examples. Fiscal decentralization was justified under the efficiency condition of fiscal expenditure, and the fiscal expenditure and management of regional units became crucial.

3. Own-Sourcism and General Resourcism

Although local autonomy was revived in 1995, a centralized structure persisted in intergovernmental fiscal relations, leading to a continued weakness in the structure of local revenue. Despite the continuous growth in the scale of local finance, the fiscal independence index and Fiscal autonomy Index remained low. One of the key financial challenges in self-government and decentralization is to enhance the general resources of local government. However, there is a difference in the understanding among local governments regarding which revenue source should be central to improving fiscal indicators.

There is a conflict between own-sourcism and general resourcism in expanding Local Finance and promoting fiscal decentralization. The former advocates revenue expansion through local tax, while the latter emphasizes the expansion of local share tax as an alternative. Local governments with a solid tax base, such as Seoul and Gyeonggi, tend to prefer own-sourcism. In contrast, municipalities with a weak foundation in local tax revenue focus on expanding local share tax as a source of funding for fiscal projects.

Local tax and local share tax create a trade-off relationship in local revenue. Based on own-sourcism, when some of the national tax is transferred to local tax, the internal tax revenue diminishes, leading to a decrease in revenue for the general share tax. To address the imbalance in general resources between financially advanced and underdeveloped regions, it is necessary to introduce a system that adjusts a portion of local tax transfers to favor underdeveloped areas. In this case, the adjustment function of local tax is strengthened, potentially weakening the core principle of own-sourcism.

4. History of Fiscal Decentralization

There has been extensive central government control over the functions of local governments. Reforms in intergovernmental relations are often influenced more by practical financial considerations and the direct interests of individual local governments rather than logical or theoretical reasoning. South Korea faces a complex reality where it needs to effectively design and operate fiscal relations similar to U.S.-style federalism within the framework of Japanese-style intergovernmental relations.

Since the revival of local autonomy in 1995, self-government and decentralization has been a central national agenda. Each government administration has introduced various policy measures to expand Self-government and decentralization. They have legislated administrative organizations and enacted relevant laws. Several innovations have been pursued to achieve fiscal decentralization as well. The simultaneous pursuit of self-government and decentralization and fiscal decentralization began during the Kim Dae-jung Administration. The Presidential Commission for Promotion of Local Empowerment was established, and the legal rate of local share tax was increased to 15% of internal tax, resulting in a net increase in local revenue.

The administration that elevated the status of self-government and decentralization to the highest level in national agendas was the Roh Moo-hyun government. It simultaneously pursued national balanced development, self-government and decentralization, and Government Innovation. The President's Commission actively drove these innovations. Notable achievements in balanced development and self-government and decentralization included the relocation of the administrative capital, the transfer of public institutions to local governments, and the establishment of Jeju special self-governing province. Regarding fiscal decentralization, key initiatives included the decentralization share tax, the differential subsidy ratio system, and the establishment of the special account for balanced national development.

<Table 9-1> Basic Principles and Institutionalization of Self-Government and Decentralization Since the Revival of Local Autonomy

	Kim Dae-jung Administration	Roh Moo-hyun Administration	Lee Myung-bak Administration	Park Geun-hye Administration	Moon Jae-in Administration (proposed)
Office Transfer Promotion Organization	Presidential Commission for Promotion of Local Transfer	Government Innovation Local Decentralization Committee; Presidential Commission for Promotion of Local Empowerment	Committee for Promoting Local Decentralization	Committee on Self-Government and Decentralization	Committee on Self-Government and Decentralization (Local Transfer Cost Assessment Committee)
Related Laws	Act on Promotion of National Administration Authority to the Local Government	Special Act on Decentralization	Special Law on Promotion of Local Decentralization	Special Law on Local Self-Government and Decentralization, and Local Administrative System Reform	Local Collective Transfer Act
Characteristics	Establishment of Initial Legal Basis	Implementation of Local Decentralization Roadmap	Reorganization of Administrative Categories	Centralization of Power Strengthening	Proposal for National Tax-Local Tax 7:3 for Constitutional Amendment on Decentralization
Major Function Transfers	Resident Autonomy Center	Jeju Special Self-Governing Province		Central Agreement on Welfare Services	Decentralization at the Federal Level
Fiscal Decentralization	15% Increase in Local Share Tax Legal Rate	• Decentralization Share Tax • Special Account for Regional Development • Differential Subsidy Ratio	• Local Consumption Tax • Coexistent Local Development Fund	• Expansion of Local Consumption Tax • Adjustment for Reduction of Acquisition Tax	• National Tax Transfer (Expansion of Local Consumption Tax) • Local Revenue Net Increase • National Subsidy Local Transfer • Adjustment for Reduction of Share Tax • Establishment of Local Extension Reaction Fund

The Lee Myung-bak and Park Geun-hye Administrations maintained the basic principles of self-government and decentralization but did not achieve significant institutional reforms or outcomes. They fundamentally upheld the centralized system of governance.

The Moon Jae-in Administration, on the other hand, introduced the concept of a decentralized state at the federal level as a national agenda. It explicitly mentioned the goal of a national tax-local tax ratio of 7:3 in its policy agenda, clearly demonstrating its commitment to fiscal decentralization. While promoting self-government and decentralization, the administration prioritized fiscal considerations and introduced new finance adjustment systems like the local extension reaction fund.

Section 2 Decentralization Share Tax

1. Significance of the Decentralization Share Tax System

The Decentralization Share Tax(DST) was introduced in 2005 to provide financial support for the Local Transfer of 149 central government-assisted projects. The funding amounted to 0.94% of internal tax. It operated for ten years on a temporary basis and was integrated into the general share tax in 2015. The financial neutrality principle ensured that the expansion of the local share tax corresponded to the scale of local transfer for central government-assisted projects, resulting in no net increase in local finance. The local transfer of central government-assisted projects was expected to bring about decentralization reforms and curb the inefficiency of such projects.

During the administration of President Roh Moo-hyun, which prioritized balanced development and local decentralization as key national agendas, the Presidential Committee on government innovation & decentralization played a central role in promoting policies related to the local transfer of central government-assisted projects and

<Table 9-2> Status of Local Transfer Project Demand by Central Ministries

(Unit: Number, million won, %)

By Ministry or Department	Total		Current Demand		Non-Current Demand	
	Number of Projects	Size of Transfer	Number of Projects	Size of Transfer	Number of Projects	Size of Transfer
Ministry of Health and Welfare	67	595,854	50	472,242	17	123,612
Ministry of Land, Infrastructure, and Transport	7	133,078			7	133,078
Ministry of Interior and Safety	4	74,157	1	49,930	3	24,227
Culture Heritage Administration	2	41,032	2	41,032		
Ministry of Culture, Sports and Tourism	24	35,628	7	24,502	17	11,126
Ministry of Agriculture, Forestry, and Fisheries	9	22,216	4	20,941	5	1,275
Ministry of Oceans and Fisheries	16	15,679	2	3,626	14	12,053
Rural Development Administration	9	10,237	6	8,518	3	1,719
Ministry of Environment	5	9,046			5	9,046
Ministry of Gender Equality and Family	2	7,532	1	7,132	1	400
Ministry of Patriots and Veterans Affairs	1	6,378			1	6,378
Ministry of Employment and Labor	1	6,092			1	6,092
Korea Forest Service	2	1,120	1	720	1	400
Total	149	958,049	74	628,643	75	329,406

Source: Kim & Lee(2008).

the expansion of local finance. To facilitate the local transfer of central government-assisted projects, the committee reclassified 533 projects worth KRW 12.7 trillion into decentralization share tax, special account for balanced national development, and national subsidy based on the extent of restrictions on the use of subsidies.

The government innovation local decentralization committee, following the 2003 "National Subsidy Reorganization Plan," transferred 163 projects(KRW 1.1 trillion) to local governments and 126 projects(KRW 3.6 trillion) to the special account for balanced national development in 2004. Among the projects eligible for local transfer, those under the Ministry of Health and Welfare accounted for 67 projects, or 45%, with related funding at KRW 595.9 billion, approximately 62.2%. Seventeen non-core projects with unstable financial demand represented 21% of the budget. Many issues arising from the implementation of the decentralization share tax system were concentrated in this area.

2. Funding and Allocation Method for DST

Decentralization share tax(DST) is part of the local share tax system, along with general share tax and special share tax. It operates based on the autonomy of local governments, and budget planning and execution are carried out autonomously by the local authorities. However, because it also allocates funds to general share tax and non-general share tax local governments, it was managed as a separate item under local share tax. The provision of funds as a general resource allowed local governments to flexibly operate central government-assisted projects that had been transferred to them.

The Ministry of Interior and Safety categorized local transfer projects into current demand and non-current demand based on their nature and calculated the allocation of funds to local governments accordingly. To secure the necessary funding for the transfer of central government-assisted projects to local authorities, various factors were considered, including the direction of national financial management, the revision of local tax laws, and more.

As part of this process, the local share tax rate was adjusted upward by 0.83% of internal tax, resulting in 8,454 billion won (88%) being secured for local transfer projects. Additionally, out of the increased revenue from the tobacco consumption tax, 1,127 billion won (12%) was earmarked for local transfer projects. Starting from 2006, when the revenue from the tobacco consumption tax turned out to be lower than expected, an additional allocation of 0.11% from internal tax was made to address the shortage of funds for decentralization share tax projects.

3. Key Issues Regarding the DST

Issues with the DST as Local Transfer System

The introduction of the decentralization share tax system in line with the Participatory Government's roadmap for local decentralization aimed to promote a decentralized national construction. However, it is evaluated that the expected decentralization innovation effects were not achieved. Financial conflicts between the central and local governments occurred from the early stages of implementing the system. Most notably, local government participation was excluded from discussions on local transfer in government-assisted projects, leading to unintended side effects of top-down decentralization innovation. This resulted in a prioritization of bureaucratic and expert "decentralization expectations" over the perspective of the "citizen's point of view."

The controversy surrounding local financial contributions in welfare assistance programs worsened due to fiscal conflicts between the central and local governments. This entrenched social criticism of both welfare and decentralization. Based on 2009 data, Seo Jeong-seop confirmed that approximately 1.1 trillion won of local financial contributions occurred after the implementation of Local Transfer. Initially, the medium-term plans predicting the expansion of welfare finance expenditure and expenditure demand variables were not considered in the estimation process of funding sources.

There was a failure to consider the fragmented difference between self-government and decentralization and fiscal decentralization. From the perspective of self-government and decentralization, an increase in the financial size and the number of financial projects of local governments can be interpreted positively. In the case of fiscal Decentralization, it is important for local governments to secure qualitative authority transfer with minimal central intervention and program-based local transfers to gain autonomy and responsibility in relevant financial projects.

As long as a vertical governmental relationship allowing central administrative intervention is maintained, and local transfer occurs at the budgetary unit level of financial projects, the centralized system persists. Local governments end up with the contradictory situation of being obligated only to share funding responsibilities for the transferred financial projects, even though the numbers suggest decentralization. In the case of local transfer in welfare assistance programs through decentralization share tax, a typical contradictory situation arose in practice.

Financial Trauma and Policy Implications

The financial trauma resulting from the decentralization share tax system negatively impacting local revenue is expected to persist for a considerable period. Consequently, local perspectives on local transfer and fiscal decentralization innovations in government-assisted projects are likely to start from a critical standpoint. This is firmly situated in the historical context where conflicts in intergovernmental fiscal relationships are likely to surface during the process of restructuring.

To reform intergovernmental fiscal relationships into a decentralization innovation, it is crucial to reform welfare assistance programs, which account for more than half of the national subsidy. However, concerns arise that the issues raised by welfare assistance programs in the context of decentralization share tax local transfer may recur, leading both central and local governments to adopt critical stances on decentralization. The critical lessons from decentralization share tax should serve as a prerequisite for the local transfer of government-assisted programs.

Section 3 Balanced Regional Development Special Account(BRD-SA)

1. Significance of the BRD-SA

Since 2005, the Ministry of Economy and Finance has been operating the special account for balanced regional development (referred to as "Special Account for Regional Development" in Korean) to promote specialized development based on regional characteristics and comparative advantages, as well as to pursue projects aimed at improving the quality of life for local residents and enhancing regional competitiveness. The name of this special account has changed over the years with different administrations.

In 2005, during the administration of President Roh Moo-hyun, decentralization was set as a core national policy objective and pursued under the banner of government innovation. A total of 149 national assistance programs were transferred to local governments through the decentralization share tax. Additionally, a special account for balanced national development was established, primarily focusing on small-scale national assistance programs related to regional development.

During President Lee Myung-bak's Administration, the special account for balanced national development was restructured and renamed as the special account for metropolitan and regional development. This reformation included the incorporation of additional government projects within its financial scope and a shift in focus from "balance" to "regional" development.

Under President Park Geun-hye's Administration, the account's name was changed to the special account for regional development.

[Figure 9-2] Special Account for Balanced Regional Development(2005)

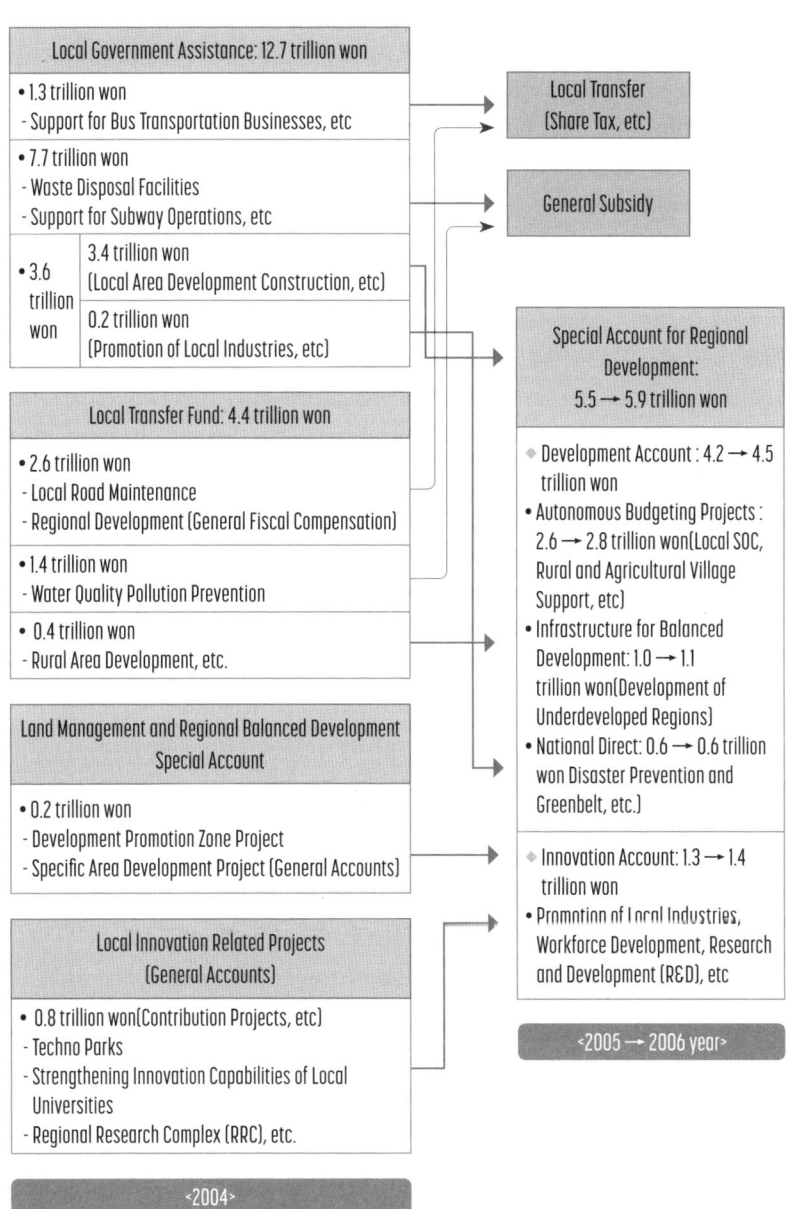

Chapter 9 — Fiscal Decentralization and Intergovernmental Relations

However, the fundamental approach of the account remained largely unchanged.

During President Moon Jae-in's Administration, in 2018, the name special account for balanced national development was reinstated, emphasizing the concept of "balance" once again. Nevertheless, the operational framework of the previous regional development special account was retained.

2. Operational Framework

The special account for regional development consists of four separate accounts. From the perspective of fiscal decentralization, the local autonomous account is of particular importance. This account integrates over 100 small-scale assistance programs that were previously managed by individual ministries. It allocates funds to local governments in lump sums, allowing them autonomy in selecting individual projects through a block grant program.

Local governments have gained autonomy in the allocation of funds for projects within the account. However, the management of individual financial projects still follows the same centralized government assistance methods as before, administered by the relevant central government ministries. From the perspective of local government budget departments, Fiscal decentralization provides autonomy, but the project departments must adhere to the same operational framework as before, leading to duplicated efforts in negotiating project funding with both central ministries and local budget departments.

In the case of the local autonomous account within the special account for regional development, the Ministry of Economy and Finance oversees revenue budgeting, while projects are managed by various ministries within the central government, following a modified block grant system. The local support account's projects are directly budgeted by the ministries. By grouping individual projects into block grants and allocating the total budget amount, it becomes possible to manage the pressure for budget increases based on the activities of beneficiary groups for each assistance program. However, in practice, delegating performance management systems to the original responsible ministries for each project within the expenditure sector may prevent the full advantages of the block grant from being realized. This can result in a more complex system of individual assistance programs, particularly when budget allocation remains unstable.

3. Implications of the BRD-SA and Fiscal Decentralization

The special account for regional development serves as a financial mechanism to promote national balanced development through the lens of fiscal decentralization. However, there is a misalignment between the symbolic or institutional values and the actual operational realities of the system, primarily due to the limited activation of proactive values.

This unique fiscal system involves direct intervention by the central budget authority, the Ministry of Economy and Finance, in the specific operation of national assistance programs. South Korea is characterized by a small government and a strong emphasis on fiscal health. The primary management objectives of the central budget authority regarding financial projects are expenditure restraint and the efficiency of financial project management. The values of performance generation and problem-solving pursued by financial projects take a back seat.

In the local autonomous account of the special account for regional development, local governments autonomously allocate funds for individual projects within the allocated total budget range. However, the supervision and management of individual projects are entrusted to various ministries within the central government. The National Assembly budget deliberation concerning revenue-related matters of the special account for regional development falls under the jurisdiction of the Strategy and Finance Committee. However, for individual projects' expenditure, each respective Standing Committee

<Table 9-5> Special Account for Balanced National Development Accounting Structure

Organizational Method	Account	Local Autonomous Account	Local Support Account	Sejong Special Self-Governing City Account	Jeju Special Self-Governing Province Account
Local Government Autonomous Formation	Metropolitan Cities·Provinces	① Municipal and Provincial Autonomous Budgeting Projects	-	③ Municipal and Provincial, Cities, Counties, and Districts Autonomous Budgeting Projects	④ Unicipal and Provincial, Cities, Counties, and Districts Autonomous Budgeting Projects * Including City, County, and District-based Development Projects
	City·County·District	② Cities, Counties, and Districts Autonomous Budgeting Projects		* Including City, County, and District-based Development Projects	⑤ Expenses for Carrying out Duties Transferred to Special Local Administrative Agencies
Direct Ministry Formation		-	⑥ Ministry-Direct Formation Projects	⑦ Ministry-Direct Formation Projects	⑧ Ministry-Direct Formation Projects

is responsible. The central government ministries and the National Assembly Standing Committees review only the content of entrusted projects without the authority to allocate funds. Within the budget proposals of each central government ministry, the special account for regional development projects are managed as separate items. As a result, a complex accounting structure is formed, making it difficult to comprehensively manage the performance of projects within the overall framework of budget projects.

Since individual projects are also included in the performance management systems of the relevant ministries, local governments must undergo performance monitoring and management by the ministries responsible for the projects under the Ministry of Economy and Finance. Since local autonomy in expenditure operations is not recognized, the term "Block Grant" is used based on the autonomy of revenue allocation. However, the block grants currently used in the United States, for example, emphasize performance management in expenditure rather than Revenue. Therefore, the block grants in the special account for regional development differ from the block grant programs operated by the U.S. federal government.

During President Moon Jae-in's Administration, amid the restructuring of the national tax-local tax 7:3 ratio, there was simultaneous progress in the transfer of national tax to local tax and the local transfer of government assistance programs. In this process, the local autonomous account projects of the special account for regional development saw significant local transfers. However, from 2023 onwards, the Ministry of Economy and Finance has continued to expand itemized projects within this account while maintaining a similar level and operating approach as in the past.

[Figure 9-3] Operational Structure of Block Grants for Local Autonomous Account Projects in the Special Account for Regional Development

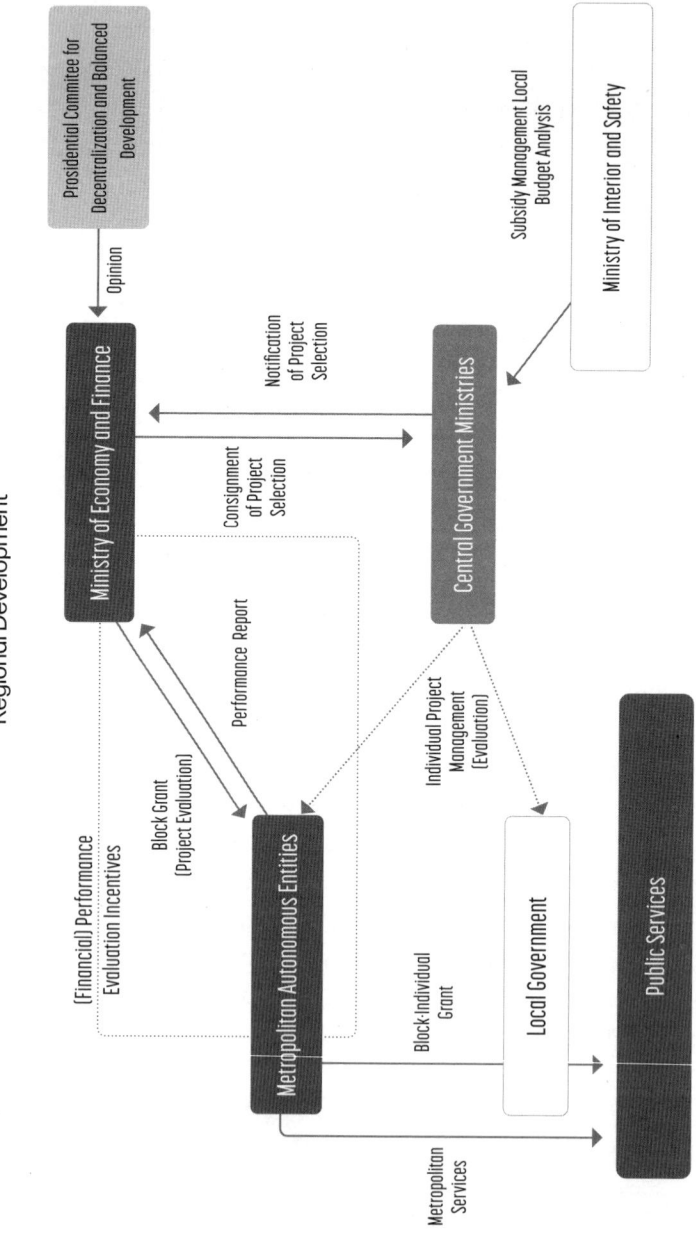

Section 4 The Transfer of National Tax to Local Tax

1. The Moon Jae-in Administration's Initiative

During the Moon Jae-in Administration, the proposal of achieving a decentralized state at the federal level was a prominent election promise. To put this into action, the administration introduced the concept of a "Decentralized State" into the constitution through Article 1, Paragraph 3, of a constitutional amendment bill submitted to the National Assembly in 2018. As part of the 100 major national tasks, one of the objectives was to adjust the National Tax-Local Tax ratio to 7:3 during the presidential term. In previous administrations, the expansion of local finance had been more symbolically incorporated into national policy objectives.

The Moon Jae-in Administration's commitment to fiscal decentralization is notable because it specified concrete numerical targets. A task force composed of various government departments was established to drive the adjustment of the national tax-local tax ratio to 7:3, with the Presidential Committee on autonomy and decentralization, self-government, and decentralization taking the lead. The process of fiscal decentralization, with a focus on the transfer of the local consumption Tax portion from the national tax, began in late 2017 and was divided into two phases, with the first phase extending into early 2023.

2. Two-Stage Fiscal Decentralization

To achieve the restructuring of the national tax-local tax ratio to 7:3, it was necessary to transfer approximately 20 trillion won of national tax to local tax, based on the 2017 standards. The fiscal decentralization plan developed by relevant government departments was divided into two stages.

The first stage aimed to transfer 10% of the total amount of

<Table 9-6> Fiscal Decentralization under the Moon Jae-in Administration: First and Second Stages

(A) Key Points of the First-Stage Fiscal Decentralization(As of 2020)

Stage 1 Fiscal Decentralization (8.5 trillion won)				
Local Tax Augmentation: Transfer 10% of Value-Added Tax 10% to Local Consumption Tax (4% in 2019, 6% in 2020)				
Priority Allocation of Local Consumption Tax(10%) (Value-Added Tax 5.3%, Flat Rate 3 years Sunset)				Remaining Local Consumption Tax (Net Increase) (Value-Added Tax 4.7%)
Special Account for Balanced National Development Government Subsidy Project Funds Preservation due to Local Transfer(3.6 trillion won)		Adjustment of Adjustment Grant	Adjustment of Education Transfer Payment	Allocation with Regional Weighting (1:2:3) Applied Contribution from Metropolitan Area Coexistent Local Development Fund
City and Province Accounts 2.8 trillion won	City and County Accounts 0.8 trillion won	0.8 trillion won	0.1 trillion won	4.0 trillion won (Contribution from Coexistent Local Development Fund: 420 billion won)
(Note)	Net increase based on local taxes is 4.0 trillion won. Excluding the reduction in Local Share Tax, the actual Local Finance Net Increase is 2.4 trillion won. If Adjustment Grant are included in the net increase in local finance, the net increase for Stage 1 local finance amounts to 3.2 trillion won.			

(B) Key Points of the Second-Stage Fiscal Decentralization(As of 2021)

(Unit: Trillion Won)

Stage 2 Fiscal Decentralization (5.3 trillion won) Net Increase is 2.2 trillion won in scale.			
Local Finance Burden	Δ3.1	Expansion of Local Finance(①+②+③)	+5.3
		Expansion of Local Tax(①)	+4.1
Government Subsidy Project Local Transfer	Δ2.3	① Increase of Local Consumption Tax(4.3%p)	+4.1
Natural Decrease of General Share Tax	Δ0.8	② Local Extension Reaction Fund (10-year temporary Local Share Tax Expansion)	+1.0
		③ Increase in National Treasury Subsidy Rate for Basic Pension	+0.2
(Note)		Net Increase: Total of 2.2 trillion won(5.3 trillion won - 3.1 trillion won) in scale	

value-added tax, which was around 8 trillion won, into the local consumption tax. Subsequently, measures were taken to address issues related to the increase in local revenue, the local transfer of national government assistance programs, local Share tax, and fiscal compensation for education finances. After determining the scale of the local consumption tax expansion, the follow-up measures were implemented. Apart from the Local Transfer and Finance Adjustment Supplementation of the special account for regional development local autonomous account projects, which accounted for 4 trillion won, the national tax's local transfer was achieved through the increase in local revenue net.

The same approach was applied in the second stage of fiscal decentralization. It involved expanding the local consumption Tax, the local transfer of national government assistance programs, and budget adjustments for the reduction in local Share tax. Additionally, a Local Extension Reaction Fund of 1 trillion won(for a 10-year period) and an increase in the basic pension subsidy rate were introduced. The second stage also had a revenue net increase of 1.2 trillion won.

When considering both the first and second stages together, the effect of expanding local revenue was 13.8 trillion won, with 5.2 trillion won as unconditional revenue net increase. While it didn't reach the initial goal of 20 trillion won in local transfer, the increase in local tax, including the net increase, can be interpreted as a significant achievement in fiscal decentralization.

3. Characteristics and Policy Implications

The fiscal decentralization carried out during the Moon Jae-in administration had distinct characteristics that set it apart from the decentralization share tax local transfer implemented during the previous administration of President Roh Moo-hyun. It prioritized the goal of expanding local taxes before the local transfer of national government assistance programs, taking a strategic approach that differed from the normative principles based on fiscal neutrality. Consequently, it proved to be an effective approach to secure the compliance of the Ministry of Economy and Finance, which had been critical of fiscal decentralization. However, from the perspective of rational institutional reform, there are underlying issues to address.

Firstly, the top-down approach to fiscal decentralization has limitations in terms of social support and legitimacy in decentralization. While there was a significant increase in revenue net, local governments did not necessarily feel the effects, and local communities did not fully grasp the meaning and impact of fiscal decentralization. The passive stance of the Ministry of Economy and Finance, which did not acknowledge the validity of decentralization, persisted throughout the process. Addressing these policy challenges will be crucial for the future implementation of fiscal decentralization.

Secondly, the simultaneous reform of intergovernmental fiscal relations at a level commensurate with the substantial increase in local taxes was not pursued. Discussions about alternative institutional reforms, such as the decentralized state model, were only partially conducted and not thoroughly considered. Consequently, while small-scale assistance programs in the special account for regional development local autonomous account were transferred, fiscal decentralization itself did not hold significant meaning. It was more of a numerical adjustment, and there was no reform of the special account for regional development system itself. While existing projects in the special account for regional development were significantly transferred, in 2023, another set of assistance programs were introduced as account projects, similar to the previous level.

Thirdly, there were limitations in reconciling fiscal conflicts within the public sector regarding fiscal decentralization. The strengthening of the financial capabilities of metropolitan autonomous bodies resulted from the expansion of the local consumption tax and the finance adjustment system. This implied an increase in the authority of metropolitan governments within the local fiscal system. In the second stage of fiscal decentralization, local governments demanded decentralization centered around local income tax, but meaningful discussions did not progress due to tax administration issues. As local consumption tax revenue concentrated in the metropolitan area, adjustment mechanisms were strengthened. As a result, while the financial influence of the Ministry of Economy and Finance diminished, the adjustment function of the Ministry of Interior and Safety expanded. From the perspective of local governments, the change in the jurisdictional departments of fiscal governance was seen as a limited shift in fiscal centralization.

References

Anton, T.J.(1997). "New Federalism and Intergovernmental Fiscal Relationships: The Implications for Health Policy." *Journal of Health Politics, Policy and Law*, 22(3).

Bennett, R.J.(1980). *The Geography of Public Finance*, London: Methuen.

Boadway, R(2001). "Inter-Governmental Fiscal Relations: The Facilitator of Fiscal Decentralization." *Constitutional Political Economy*, 12.

Cho, Im Gon(2019). "Fiscal Decentralization and Enhancing Responsibilities of Local Government Finances in Korea." *Local Tax Review*, 6(2). (Korean)

Choe, Byeong Ho & Jeong, Jong Pil(2007). "A Study on the Share of Local Matching Funds between Upper-tier and Lower-tier Local Governments in the National Disbursement Fund." *Journal of Korean National Economy*, 25(3). (Korean)

Choi, Won Koo & Yoo, Seung Ju(2022). "A Study on the Fiscal Share of Expenses of Special-Purpose Local Government: Focusing on the Busan-Ulsan-Gyeongnam Case". *Korean Journal of Local Finance*, 27(3). (Korean)

Clark, T. & L.C. Ferguson(1983). *City Money : Political Processes, Fiscal Strain, and Retrenchment*. New York: Columbia University Press.

Esping-Andersen, G. (1999). *Social Foundations of Postindustrial Economies*. Oxford Univ. Press.

Fuchs, E.R.(1992). *Mayers and Money : Fiscal Policy in the New York and Chicago*. Chicago : The Univ. of Chicago Press.

Gadenne, L & M. Singha(2014). "Decentralization in Developing Economies." *Annual Review of Economics*, 6(1).

Ha, Neung Sik & Lee, Sun Young. *Future-oriented Normalization of Local Tax System*. Korean Institute of Local Finance. (Korean)

Joo, Man Soo(2018). "The Principle of Fiscal Decentralization and Evaluation on the Korean Local Fiscal System: The Foundation for the Fiscal Decentralization Reform." *The Korea Local Administration Review*, 32(1). (Korean).

Keum, Jaeduk(2010). "A Study on Solutions for the Problems Existing in the Financial Reporting System of South Korean Local Governments." *Journal of Governance Studies*, 5(1). (Korean).

Kim, Eui Seob(2022). "Decentralization, Asymmetric Decentralization and Regional Economic Development in Korea." *The Journal of Korean Public Policy*, 24(1). (Korean)

Kim, Hongwhan & Chung, Soon Gwan(2018). "Evaluation of Decentralization Tasks and Achievements of Past Governments." *The Korea Local Administration Review*, 32(1). (Korean).

Lee, Hyun Woo(2017). *A Study on Role of Government Type and Local Fiscal Structure in USA*. Gyonggi Development Institution. (Korean)

Lee, Jae Eun(2022). "Paradox of Fiscal Decentralization Reform in Korea." *Korean Journal of Local Finance*, 27(2). (Korean)

Lee, Jaewon(1999). *Performance Budgeting System for Local Government*. Gyeonggi Development Institute. (Korean)

Lee, Jaewon(2009). "Decentralized Management of Central Government Subsidy with Block Grant." *Korean Journal of Local Finance*, 14(1). (Korean).

Lee, Jaewon(2011). "The Role of Local Finance for the Social Service Investment." *Korean Journal of Local Finance*, 16(1). (Korean).

Lee, Jaewon(2019). "Fiscal Decentralization Initiatives and Fiscal Federalism Agenda for Building the Federal-Level Decentralized State." *Korean Journal of Local Finance*, 24(1). (Korean).

Lee, Jaewon(2019). *Local Finance*. Yoonseongsa. (Korean)

Lee, Jong Soo et al.(2014). *New Public Administration 2.0*. DYM. (Korean)

Min, Kee(2013). "A Study on the Improvement of Moral Hazard in Local

Share Tax System." *The Journal of Korean Public Policy*, 15(1). (Korean)

Muramatsu, M.(2001). "Intergovernmental Relations in Japan: Models and Perspectives." World Bank Report No 37178.

Musgrave, R.A.(1959). *The Theory of Public Finance*. McGraw-Hill.

Oates, W.E.(1972). *Fiscal Federalism*, New York: Harcourt Braco Jovanovich.

O'Connor, J. (1973), *The Fiscal Crisis of the State*, New York: St. Martin's Press.

Pai, Inmyung(2013). "A Study on the Standard Rate of Subsidies of Welfare Services." *Modern Society and Public Administration*, 23(3). (Korean)

Pammer, Jr., W.J.(1990). *Managing Fiscal Strain in Major American Cities: Understanding Retrenchment in the Public Sector*. Greenwood Press.

Park, Byeonghee(2019). "Local Governmental Fiscal Responsibility and Fiscal investment appraisal system." *Local Finance*, 2019-3. (Korean)

Pinch, S.(1985), *Cities and Services*, London: Routledge & Kegan Paul.

Ra, Hui Mun(2021). *Local Finance*. DYM (Korean)

Rhodes, R.A.W.(1997). *Understanding Governance: Policy Networks, Governance, Reflexivity and Accountability*. Open Universty Press.

Savas, E.S.(1982). *Privatizing the Public Sector*. Chatham House Publishers.

Seo Jeoung Seoup & Jo, Ki Hyun(2006). *A Study on Improving the Decentralization Revenue Sharing System in Korea*. Korea Research Institute for Local Administration. (Korean)

Sohn, Hee Jun(2019). *New Local Public Finance* DYM. (Korean)

Tiebout, C.(1956). "A Pure Theory of Local Expenditures." *Journal of Political Economy*, 64.

Weingast, B.R(1995). "The Economic Role of Political Institutions:

Market-preserving Federalism and Economic Development." *Journal of Law, Economics and Organisations*, 15(1).

Wollman, H.(2004). "Local Government Reforms in Great Britain, Sweden, Germany and France: Between Multi-Function and Single-Purpose Organizations." *Local Government Studies*, 30(4).

Won, Gu hwan(2014). "The Future of Local Public Enterprises." *The Korean Journal of Local Public Enterprises*, 10(2). (Korean)

Woo, Myoung Dong(2019). "Inclusive Growth and Local Public Finance: With Focus on Social Sustainability and Intergovernmental Fiscal Relations." *Korean Journal of Local Finance*, 24(1). (Korean)

World Bank(1999). *World Development Report 1999/2000: Entering the 21st Century—The Changing Development Landscape*. Washington, DC: World Bank.

Wright, D.S.(1988). *Understanding Intergovernment Relations*, 3rd., Brook/Co.

Yoo, Tae Hyun(2017). "Direction of Customized Fiscal Decentralization Reflecting Local Financial Condition." *Korean Journal of Local Finance*, 22(3). (Korean).

Yoo, Taekyun(2018). "Job Creation in the Social Service Sector: A Critical Review of the Current Problems and the New Administration's Policies." *Korean Journal of Social Welfare Studies*, 49(1). (Korean)

Yoon, Sungil & Lim, Dongwan(2019). "Indigenization of Participatory Budgeting." *Korean Society and Public Administration*, 29(4) (Korean)

Yoon, Young Jin(2016). *New Local Public Finance*. DYM. (Korean)

Index

A

Act on Contracts 25
Adjustment Grant 69
Autonomous District Adjustment Grants 69

B

Balanced National Development Special Account(BND-SA) 84
balanced regional development 160
Balanced Regional Development Special Account 21, 80
balancedecentralization 40
Basic Pension Act 24
Basic Plan on Gender Equality and Gender Impact Analysis 125
block grant 81, 163, 165
Building Maintenance Fund 91

C

central government 21
Centralized Project Management System 141
Central-Local Welfare Grand 146
Certificate Borrowing Goods 89
citizen's point of view 158

D

Debt 116, 120
decentralization 21, 29, 37, 98, 148
decentralization share tax 158, 160
decentralization share tax local transfer 159
Decentralization Share Tax System 155
Decentralized State 167

E

Enforcement Decree of the Subsidy Management Act 77
ESG 118

F

Financial Crisis Management 104
financial neutrality principle 155
financial shortfall 65
Fire & Security Share Tax 64
Fiscal Autonomy Index 38
Fiscal Capacity Index 40
fiscal decentralization 148, 151, 153, 162, 167, 169
fiscal independence index 37, 152
fiscal risk 103

G

Gender Budget Statement	125
Gender Budget System	124, 127
General Accounts Bonds	87
General Resource	38
General Resourcism	152
general share tax	33, 61, 65, 157
government innovation	160
government innovation & decentralization	155

I

inter-governmental relations	150
Intergovernmental Revenue	42
Inter-Governmental Welfare Finance	139

L

Local Accounting Act	25
Local Autonomy Act	22, 72, 92, 151
Local Bond Issuance	90
Local Bond Management	92
Local Bond Management System	90
Local Bonds	06, 09
local consumption tax	53, 169
Local Decentralization Roadmap	122
local education tax	54
Local Expenditure	20
Local Extinction Reaction Fund	64
Local Extinction Response Fund	61
Local Finance	19, 37, 75, 134, 136, 131
Local Finance Act	73, 92, 98, 121, 122
Local Finance Adjustment System	27, 37
Local Finance Analysis System	103
Local Finance Investment Review	101
Local Finance Management	20
Local Financial Impact Assessment	101
Local Fiscal Management	98, 105
Local Fiscal Management System	96
Local General Revenue	143
local government	21, 22, 26, 52
Local Government Expenditure	33
local government finance management system	21
Local Government Fund	25
Local Government Revenue	31
Local Government Type	33
Local Governments	92
Local Grant	128
Local Grant Budget	129
Local Grant Budget Management	128
Local Grant Review Committee	129
Local Non-Tax Revenue	54, 58
Local Public Enterprises	25, 118, 111, 114
Local Public Enterprises Act	24, 108

Local Public Enterprises
Management Evaluation 118
Local Public Fee Stabilization
Incentive System 116
Local Revenue 20, 23, 31
local share tax 23, 24, 33, 60, 66, 152
local tax 23, 50, 52, 152, 165
Local Tax Act 24
Local Tax Non-Local Resources 54
Local Taxes 41, 45
Local Transfer System 158

M

Management Evaluation System 119
Management Innovation 118
Management of Public Institutions Act 101
Mid-term Local Finance Plan 96

N

National Finance Act 124, 127
National Health Insurance Service 147
National Pension Management Service 145
national subsidy 75
National Subsidy Projects 75, 77
National Subsidy Reorganization Plan 157
National Subsidy Source 75
National Subsidy Trends 76
national tax 152, 165

National Tax-Local Tax Revenue Share 49
new social risks 134
non-general share tax 157

O

ordinary tax 71

P

Participatory Budgeting 121
Post-Fiscal Management 103
Pre-Budget System 100
Principle of No Taxation Without Law 52
Public Enterprise Special Account Bonds 87
Public Fees 116
Public Property 25

R

Real Estate Share Tax 33, 63
Real-name Business System 119
Regional Coexistent Development Fund(RCDF) 69, 71, 74, 84
Regional Development Public Bonds 90

S

Security Issue Bonds 89
self-government 37, 149, 153, 159, 167
Social Welfare Expenditure 131

special account for balanced national development 153, 160
special account for regional development 163
special share tax 33, 61, 157
Standard Subsidy Rate 144
subsidies 24, 77
subsidized projects 105
Subsidy 75, 82, 105
Subsidy Management Act
23, 24, 107, 144
Subsidy Project System 107

T

Tax Price Principle 50
Taxation Sovereignty 52
The Local Finance Act 23
The Mid-term Local Finance Plan
100
Tiebout Hypothesis 149
tobacco consumption tax 158
total amount of value-added tax 42

U

Urban Railway Bonds 89

W

Welfare Decentralization 134
Welfare Finance 143
Women's Budget 125

Korean Local Finance

About the Authors

B. Shine Cho

Professor, Konkuk University, Department of Public Administration

Hyungjo Hur

Professor, Dankook University, Department of Public Administration

Jaewon Lee

Professor, Pukyong National University, Division of Public Administration and Social Welfare

Korean Local Finance